'70s
CHICAGOLAND
ROCK CONCERTS

'70s CHICAGOLAND
ROCK CONCERTS

CONCERT PHOTOS BY **JIM SUMMARIA**

STORIES BY **MARK PLOTNICK**

THE
History
PRESS

Published by The History Press
Charleston, SC
www.historypress.com

Front cover: Pete Townshend, the Who, 1975.
Back cover: Paul McCartney, Wings, 1976.
Backstage collage, page 281: *Courtesy of Rich Currier*.

First published 2024

Manufactured in the United States

ISBN 9781467156851

Library of Congress Control Number: 2024941879

The '70s, undeniably the most significant decade in Chicagoland rock history, captured on film and presented here to rekindle old memories or show you what you missed. Jim's pictures and Mark's words really take me back to those great old days. Every picture tells a story.
—Larry Rosenbaum, co-founder/owner of Flip Side Productions

The '70s were so incredible. The music was literally "off the charts," and the live performances were even more outrageous. I think back to shows from places like the Uptown, Auditorium Theatre, the Aragon, the Park West, the old Chicago Stadium, the International Amphitheater, Soldier Field and old Comiskey Park. Jim and Mark's pictures and words will take you back to that remarkable decade. Enjoy the ride.
—Mitch Michaels, Chicago radio legend

The 1970s were a great era for almost any genre of music heard around the world. The epicenter for many of those genres was right here in Illinois. Jim Summaria captures the essence of that era with his photos, and Mark Plotnick describes what you see in a way that draws you into those historic moments as if we stood right there, right then, where the photos were taken.
—Ron Romero, CEO/founder of the Illinois Rock & Roll Museum on Route 66

As a founding member of Climax Blues Band and having had the privilege of touring the USA during the '70s and '80s with the best of the best, it's wonderful to see this incredible collection of action photos of great artists and gigs that personifies the era I was involved with. Jim's incredible images coupled with Mark's in-depth bios, dates, venues and setlists make this an up close and personal visual journey and informative insight into the "Golden Days" and wonderful world of rock concerts. This book takes you right back there!
—Derek Holt, Climax Blues Band

I dedicate this book to my wonderful family for all their love and support, my wife, Sheila; son, Michael; daughter, Melissa; and son-in-law, Logan.
Jim Summaria

This book is dedicated to my patient, supportive and loving wife, Hope; my folks, Lillian and Sam Plotnick, who believed in me when I didn't and who'd be proud if alive today; and to my uncles LTC Jerry Sacks and Bob Sacks (my mother's beloved brothers), who passed away too young for me to fully enjoy what they meant to me.
—Mark Plotnick

CONTENTS

Contents

INTRODUCTIONS

JIM SUMMARIA

Growing up in the 1950s, music was always in our house. My parents played Frank Sinatra and the big bands on the hi-fi, and my brother spun Elvis, Chuck Berry, Jerry Lee Lewis and Little Richard on his record player. I developed my own tastes in music by listening to the radio (WLS in Chicago, of course, and particularly Dick Biondi) with my sister. Bands like the Four Seasons and the Beach Boys were early favorites.

But in early 1964, I heard a song that changed me forever. That song was "I Want to Hold Your Hand" by the Beatles. And on February 9, 1964, I was transfixed along with seventy-three million viewers watching the Beatles on *The Ed Sullivan Show*. The British invasion had begun, and the Rolling Stones, the Dave Clark Five and the Animals followed with their brand of rock music. I now couldn't get enough of rock 'n' roll.

When I was twelve, in 1966, my sister took me to my first concert at the International Amphitheater in Chicago. I saw the Turtles, the Young Rascals, Mitch Ryder & the Detroit Wheels and the Gentrys. I was hooked on live music! My next concert was the Monkees in 1967 at the International Amphitheater. I brought my Kodak Instamatic camera with flash cube and have a great photo of the back of the heads of the people in the row in front of me. Ha!

My music tastes expanded when I first heard "Sunshine of Your Love" by Cream in 1967 and "Fire" by the Jimi Hendrix Experience. My journey continued when I heard the long version of The Doors' "Light My Fire." The song heightened my senses. Another important rock moment happened in late 1969 when I first heard Led Zeppelin playing on my friend's 8-track player. A total OMG moment.

In 1971, my friends Gary, Paco and I saw Black Sabbath at the Auditorium Theatre. My god, they were loud! My god, I loved it! We started buying tickets for nearly every concert in the Chicagoland area.

One more key moment in my musical journey happened in March 1972 when we saw Long John Baldry, Fleetwood Mac (post Peter Green) and Savoy Brown for The British Are Coming tour. This blues-filled concert—especially the set by Kim Simmonds and Savoy Brown—turned me on to the blues and later led me to such artists as Muddy Waters, B.B. King and others.

In 1972, I brought my Kodak Instamatic camera to a Rolling Stones concert at the International Amphitheater. We had tenth-row center seats, and I took eleven blurry shots and one halfway decent picture. I was hooked on taking photos at concerts. Soon I graduated to a 35mm film camera with a telephoto lens, and my photos got better, which led to shooting for Flip Side Records and the photographs in this book. I hope my photos bring back fond memories of a few of the many great concerts in the Chicagoland area in the 1970s.

MARK PLOTNICK

My love affair with music arrived in stages. It began in the late 1950s with my parents' then state-of-the-art audio separates from Allied Radio. That system could kick out the jams! For my folks, those jams included philharmonic orchestras, Strauss waltzes, movie soundtracks and mariachi and klezmer music. Nothing grabbed me other than Jewish clarinetist Mickey Katz.

When I was around age nine (1959), my folks bought a Kimball console piano. Little did I know how four years of typical piano lessons would influence my life. But that's another story.

My first connection with pop music arrived around 1961. My uncle Jerry gifted me a portable battery-powered reel-to-reel recorder with speaker. I was fascinated with the ability to record and listen to my favorite songs repeatedly.

The British invaded us again. This time, it was Brit pop: the Beatles, Rolling Stones, Animals (my favorite), DC5, Kinks and so on. Paul Revere and the Raiders defended our turf. That Vox Continental organ was so cool, but the Hammond organ had soul.

Piano music for these acts was scarce or poorly scored—so I learned songs by ear and improvised. Several years later, I would place a Shure mic inside my piano, run it to a friend's Fender Twin Reverb amp and fantasize about performing at a large venue.

During my high school years, I drew an organizational chart diagramming rock 'n' roll music. A friend saw it and asked, "Are there really all these types?" "Where'd you get this stuff?"

My uncle Bob from Milwaukee owned a popular camera, electronics and record store. He brought me *Surrealistic Pillow* by Jefferson Airplane and an album by Love. My tastes were about to get heavier.

It started with those bluesy, psychedelic garage rock bands. Then I touched the monolith: Eric Clapton's guitar playing with John Mayall's Bluesbreakers.

One night, that rock 'n' roll monolith reappeared. My bedside clock radio blasted out "Purple Haze" by the Jimi Hendrix Experience. At first, my ears were confused—but I knew I liked it. Other guitar gods followed.

I became a Cream fanatic, which led to my discovery of authentic blues musicians. The Doors came next and later, the Allman Brothers Band, ZZ Top and Lynyrd Skynyrd. I was obsessed with southern rock. Most unusual for a kid of my background. But my tastes also grew to embrace singer-songwriters: Joni Mitchell, Cat Stevens, Gordon Lightfoot and more.

Simultaneously, I dove headfirst into space rock, particularly Pink Floyd. And the jazz-rock fusion of the Mahavishnu Orchestra nearly exploded my brain.

My first concert was the Jefferson Airplane in 1968 at Chicago's Aragon Ballroom. Gracie was hot. While I was away at college, Steppenwolf and Led Zeppelin II were blasting out of dorm rooms. The Vietnam War sharpened my senses for bands like Crosby, Stills, Nash and Young: "Tin soldiers and Nixon coming…"

In my early twenties, I made dozens of cassette tapes for my aftermarket car cassette player. I rushed back and forth between my car and home stereo to get each tape equalized just right. The car was my music listening sanctuary.

Throughout my higher education, music interrupted my studies. It closed one career door, but thankfully, others always opened.

Now that I am seventy-four, music keeps me thinking young. It inhabits my brain. It pulls me out of funks. My longtime friend Jim Summaria pulled me out of retirement shortly after it began and gave my passion a new outlet. Jim feels the music like I do. That's why our friendship is special and why we do these books. Hope you feel the joy.

ACKNOWLEDGEMENTS

JIM SUMMARIA

So many people have influenced me throughout my life. Here are but a few who have helped me personally and professionally: my parents, Enrico and Angelina; my brother, Joe; my sister, Cynthia; my friends; my relatives; Tom Caprile; Ed Siena; Mark Clark; Mark Plotnick; Marc Fleming; Gary Kubowicz; Cher Connelly; Marv Chait; John Mendicino; Bill Decker; Terry House; Rich Carlson; Larry Rosenbaum; Carl Rosenbaum; Dave Slania; Mike Calcina; Shawn O'Malley; Mike Schmitt; Gerry Hurley; Mark Anderson; Lou Bilotti; Ron Onesti; Lisa Torem; and my softball teammates, players and coaches. And for their inspiration: Diane Arbus, Jim Marshall, Annie Leibovitz, Yousuf Karsh, Mary Ellen Mark, Bruce Dale, Jim McCurry and Victor Skrebneski. Also Rich Currier for supplying me with his backstage passes.

MARK PLOTNICK

My "resting in peace" friends Alan Day and Joe Perri, my very much alive friends Jim Summaria, Ed Siena, Dean Carlstone, Alan Cohn, Tom Lasken, Terry Grider, Robert Van Tuyle and others. To all of my guitar idols who play those riffs that make me smile. To the late blues pianist Otis Spann, whom I didn't realize I was trying to emulate (poorly) until someone in my college dorm heard me play and said, "You need to listen to Otis Spann and work on your left hand." Still do! To the Return of the Flock band for lifting my spirits whenever they perform and for just being nice guys. To veteran radio personality Mitch Michaels, who was the first to interview us about our first book. And to Jim Eggers, who gave us our first shot at a radio show, and to those guests who felt we were worthy enough to appear.

THE ROLLING STONES

FORMED 1963

BAND MEMBERS WHO MATTER

Mick Jagger (lead vocals, harmonica, guitar), Keith Richards (guitar, vocals), Brian Jones (guitar, other instruments), Bill Wyman (bass, vibraphone), Charlie Watts (drums), Mick Taylor (guitar), Ronnie Wood (guitar, vocals).

> TOUR MANAGER SAM CUTLER: Everything seems to be ready... are you ready for the next band? We are sorry for the delay....Is everybody ready? The biggest band to visit New York...the Rolling Stones...the Rolling Stones...The greatest rock 'n' roll band in the world...the Rolling Stones...the Rolling Stones...

WHY THEY MATTER

...the crowd erupts! And so goes the introduction to "Jumpin' Jack Flash" from the live 1969 album *Get Yer Ya-Ya's Out!* Jagger resented the "greatest rock 'n' roll band in the world" label. Jagger told *Rolling Stone* magazine, "It's just a stupid epithet. It just seems too Barnum and Bailey to me. It's so embarrassing."

But if any band deserved such hyperbole, it is the Rolling Stones. In a live setting, the Stones set a new standard for swagger and get-dirty rock 'n' roll that has stood the test of time. No band has done more to define the

Above: Mick Jagger. *Opposite:* Keith Richards.

look, attitude and sound than the Stones. No rock 'n' roll shrine would be complete without the band's "tongue and lips" logo.

Jagger and Richards have the longest-running songwriting and performing partnership ever. No music act has performed for more people worldwide, and none has grossed more than the Stones. Even when essential second guitar duties moved from Brian Jones to Mick Taylor to Ronnie Wood, the Stones never missed a beat.

The band's origins date to October 17, 1961, when two teens from Dartford, England, crossed paths at a Dartford railway station and bonded over music. Through a series of events, they came across a blues-loving young man (Brian Jones) from Cheltenham sitting in with Alex Korner Blues Incorporated. A month or so later, Richards entered a SoHo pub and heard the impressive boogie-woogie piano played by a Scotsman named Ian Stewart. Although never officially a Rolling Stone, Ian wore many hats and kept the boys afloat when they lived like indigents. But it was Brian Jones's inspiration, vision and chutzpah that made the Rolling Stones possible.

CHARLIE WATTS: Brian was very instrumental in pushing the band at the beginning. It was a crusade [for] him to get us on stage in a club.

On July 12, 1962, the Rollin' Stones (no -*g* at the time) played their first gig at London's Marquee Club. On drums was future Kinks stickman Mick Avory and future Pretty Things founder Dick Taylor on bass. When Taylor departed, Bill Wyman (birth name William Perks) came aboard. He was years older than his future bandmates and had served in the British Royal Air Force. Laughably, his future bandmates were more interested in his equipment than his playing ability.

Charlie Watts was long sought to be the band's drummer, but he liked the steady paycheck from graphic design work and gigs with Alex Korner. After some convincing, Watts joined Wyman as one of rock's tightest rhythm sections. By February 1963, the band was complete.

KEITH RICHARDS: Number one with Charlie is that he's got great feel. He had it from the start. There's tremendous personality and subtlety in his playing. Even if I can't hear him, I can play by just watching him.

In April 1963, Andrew Loog Oldham entered the picture as manager and producer. He devised the band's "dangerous and unkempt" image and made three key moves: (1) secured a Decca Records contract, (2) pushed Ian Stewart to the sidelines and (3) urged Jagger and Richards to write their own material.

In 1966, the Stones released *Aftermath*, their first LP with all original songs. Attention and influence shifted from Brian Jones to Jagger and Richards. Brian's forte was adding color and tone thanks to his eclectic musical influences and instrumental versatility.

BILL WYMAN: Brian would walk into a studio and no matter what instrument was lying around—even though he'd never played it before—would be able to knock something out of it very quickly.

Let It Bleed was the last album to feature serious contributions by Jones. His last live appearance as a Rolling Stone took place in December 1968 for the *Rolling Stones Rock and Roll Circus*. By then, Jones had become unstable and unfocused. He was obsessed with looks, celebrity and hobnobbing. One day in June 1969, Jagger, Richards and Watts delivered the bad news.

MICK JAGGER: It wasn't pleasant, but it had to be done. He wouldn't come to the studio. He couldn't hold the guitar. In fact, we came to a point where we couldn't play live because Brian was a total liability.

A month later, Brian Jones was found dead in his swimming pool. A few days later, the Stones put on a free concert in London's Hyde Park dedicated to Brian. The concert also introduced the Stone's new guitarist Mick Taylor. At the age of sixteen, Taylor rose to fame with John Mayall's Bluesbreakers.

Mick Taylor was no ordinary guitarist. Fans, critics and even band members contend that the Rolling Stones were at their pinnacle during the Taylor years (1969–74). After the release of *It's Only Rock 'n' Roll*, Taylor unexpectedly quit the band. Multiple factors led to his departure, but he never intended to be a Rolling Stone for life.

MICK TAYLOR: I was strained and burnt out. Some of the time it was incredibly chaotic, [but] we created some of our best music. I didn't realize how much I missed being with them until we played again [2012 reunion]. Once I got on stage, I felt completely at home and very much in my element.

KEITH RICHARDS: We did the most brilliant stuff together and some of the most brilliant stuff the Stones ever did. I was in awe sometimes listening to Mick Taylor, especially to that slide.

In 1975, the Stones opened a new chapter with Ronnie Wood on second guitar. Wood looked and acted like a Stone. Before joining, Wood played bass with the Jeff Beck Group and guitar with the Faces and Rod Stewart.

RONNIE WOOD: I just looked at it like I was doing my apprenticeship. I was learning but teaching as well. During the Dirty Work album days—a really bad time—I got them through that period.

In 1985, the band lost one of its original anchors and friends. Pianist Ian Stewart suffered a heart attack. Keith Richards lamented, "Stu was the hardest hit I ever had apart from my son dying. I got really mad at him leaving me."

Like Mick Taylor, Bill Wyman had an eye on life beyond the Stones. In 1974, he was the first Stone to release a solo album. In late 1992, he made his decision: "I got to a point on our 1990 Japan tour where I didn't want to

Left to right: Ronnie Wood, Keith Richards and Charlie Watts.

fly anymore. After that, I thought, 'I've got my career, and I can do anything now.' I've always been interested in multiple things since I was a teenager. I've never been happier."

For two years, Mick, Keith and Charlie left the door open for Bill's return. In 1994, the Stones replaced Wyman with bassist Darryl Jones, who had worked with Miles Davis, Herbie Hancock and Sting.

In 2016, writer Brian Hiatt pointed out that Charlie Watts—then seventy-five years old—had the band's most physically demanding job. Keith Richards declared, "Charlie Watts will never die or retire. I forbid him."

On August 24, 2021, Charlie passed away peacefully in a London hospital.

BRIAN MAY: He was the nicest gent you could ever meet. And such a pillar of strength for the Rolling Stones—to whom he brought a touch of jazz and a mountain of pure class.

Over the years, the Rolling Stones have topped the charts around the world with an impressive number of albums that have achieved gold, silver, platinum and diamond sales certifications. Their music remains ever-present in motion picture soundtracks and high-profile advertising campaigns.

Keith Richards believes in the power of music: "You can build a wall to stop people, but eventually, the music will cross that wall....There's no defense against it. I mean, look at Joshua and Jericho. Made mincemeat of that joint with a few trumpets, you know?"

MUSICAL INFLUENCES WHO MATTER

Muddy Waters, Chuck Berry, Little Richard, Elvis Presley, Robert Johnson, Howlin' Wolf, Alexis Korner, Cyril Davies, Willie Dixon, Matt Murphy, Hubert Sumlin, B.B. King, Little Walter, Junior Wells, Bo Diddley, Scotty Moore, Jerry Lee Lewis, Fats Domino, Bill Haley, Gene Vincent, Tina Turner, Eddie Cochran, John Coltrane, Charlie Parker, Cannonball Adderley, Elvin Jones, Aretha Franklin, James Brown, Marvin Gaye, Otis Redding, Solomon Burke, Supremes, Ronettes, Crystals, Temptations, Everly Brothers.

PROBABLE CONCERT SETLIST: CHICAGO STADIUM, JULY 22, 1975

"Honky Tonk Women," "All Down the Line," "If You Can't Rock Me," "Get Off of My Cloud," "Star Star," "Gimme Shelter," "Ain't Too Proud to Beg," "You Gotta Move," "You Can't Always Get What You Want," "Happy," "Tumbling Dice," "It's Only Rock 'n' Roll," "Fingerprint File," "Wild Horses," "That's Life and Outa-Space" (performed by Billy Preston), "Brown Sugar," "Midnight Rambler," "Rip This Joint," "Street Fighting Man," "Jumpin' Jack Flash."

Opposite: Mick Jagger.

FACES

FORMED 1969

BAND MEMBERS WHO MATTER

Rod Stewart (lead vocals), Ronnie Wood (guitar, vocals), Ronnie Lane (bass, vocals), Kenney Jones (drums), Ian McLagan (keyboards).

WHY THEY MATTER

The Faces' place in rock 'n' roll history is linked to an earlier band. In the early 1960s, British youth were aligning themselves along music, fashion and lifestyle preferences. Two prominent subcultures were the mods and rockers. Three groundbreaking mod bands were the Kinks, the Who and the Small Faces. Beloved in England, the latter was primarily known in America for the trippy Summer of Love hit "Itchycoo Park."

When Small Faces singer/guitarist Steve Marriott left to form Humble Pie with Peter Frampton, the remaining members joined singer Rod Stewart and guitarist Ronnie Wood fresh from their stint with the Jeff Beck Group.

A name change followed, and the Small Faces became Faces. Between 1969 and 1975, the Faces made some of the most endearing, rollicking and quintessentially British rock 'n' roll music ever. Their songs and performances turned local pubs into listening venues on a Saturday night.

Rod Stewart.

IAN MCLAGAN: The early days were extremely shambolic, and we never wasted too much time rehearsing, especially while the pubs were still open. The tours were as mad as Marx Brothers movies. The Faces were a music-making band of characters.

That disarray certainly contributed to the band's reputation for ragged playing in later years. While Stewart and Wood gave the band muscle and moxie, Ronnie Lane's singing and songwriting gave it heart and humanity. Kenney Jones brought his disciplined drumming to the lineup while Ian McLagan's electric piano and organ provided a bluesy, honky-tonk feel.

The Faces released four solid studio albums between 1970 and 1973. *A Nod Is as Good as a Wink to a Blind Horse* soared to no. 2 in the United Kingdom and no. 6 in the United States and yielded the Faces' best-known

Ronnie Wood (*left*) and Rod Stewart.

Rod Stewart.

U.S. single, "Stay with Me." The album *Ooh La La* topped the charts in the United Kingdom.

While the Faces were well received by American audiences, Rod "The Mod" Stewart was launching his own successful parallel career with the albums *Gasoline Alley* and *Every Picture Tells a Story*. Various members of the Faces played on those albums, although credits back then were sketchy due to contractual constraints.

In 1973, Ronnie Lane jumped ship, fearing his mates had become sidemen for Rod Stewart. Ian McLagan recalled this moment as losing the band's heart and soul. From that point on, it was Rod Stewart and the Faces, with the group playing many of Stewart's own recordings onstage.

The Faces disbanded in 1975 and became more famous for what each did next. Stewart went on to become…well…Rod Stewart. Kenney Jones joined the Who, replacing the deceased Keith Moon. Ronnie Wood famously replaced Mick Taylor in the Rolling Stones, and Ian McLagan became a sought-after journeyman for studio and tour work.

Ronnie Lane never achieved the heights of his former bandmates, although his solo work was validated by his peers. One bright spot was his 1977 album, *Rough Mix*, a collaboration with Pete Townshend. Contributing artists included Eric Clapton, John Entwistle of the Who, pianist Ian Stewart and drummer Charlie Watts of the Rolling Stones.

About this time, Lane was diagnosed with multiple sclerosis. A benefit concert (1983 ARMS Charity Concert) featuring British rock royalty was put together. Sadly, Ronnie Lane succumbed to the disease in 1997.

In 2012, the Small Faces and Faces became members of the Rock & Roll Hall of Fame.

MUSICAL INFLUENCES WHO MATTER

Motown, Stax, Skiffle, Jackie Wilson, James Brown, Temptations, Four Tops, Buddy Holly, Ray Charles, Muddy Waters, Bobby "Blue" Bland, Booker T. & the M.G.'s, Shadows, Little Richard, Sam Cooke, Otis Redding, the Carter Family, Woody Guthrie.

PROBABLE CONCERT SETLIST:
CHICAGO STADIUM, OCTOBER 31, 1975

"Memphis, Tennessee," "It's All Over Now," "Miss Judy's Farm," "Three Time Loser," "I'd Rather Go Blind," "Sweet Little Rock & Roller," "(I Know) I'm Losing You," "Big Bayou," "Angel," "Bring It on Home to Me," "You Send Me," "You Wear It Well," "Maggie May," "Stay with Me," "Twistin' the Night Away."

TEN YEARS AFTER

FORMED 1967

BAND MEMBERS WHO MATTER

Alvin Lee (guitar, vocals), Leo Lyons (bass), Ric Lee (drums, percussion), Chick Churchill (piano, organ, synthesizers, backup vocals).

> DOT BARNES (ALVIN LEE'S MOTHER): He practiced every single minute he could and got on like crazy with it so quickly. It was then that I knew the talent was there and nothing could stop him.

WHY THEY MATTER

There are moments that define an act for better or worse. For the band Ten Years After (TYA), one seminal moment did both, as documented in a 1970 award-winning film *Woodstock*. It is why so many recollections of TYA begin in the middle rather than the beginning or latter part of their performing days.

On August 17, 1969, Alvin Lee, Leo Lyons, Ric Lee and Chick Churchill made it to an event that was a logistical and ecological maelstrom. The site was Max Yasgur's dairy farm in Upstate New York. The event was Woodstock.

The stage was dangerously wet when TYA appeared around eight o'clock in the evening. Weather created a multitude of technical problems, and

Alvin Lee.

Michael Wadleigh's camera crew was unable to film the band's first five songs of a six-song set. But oh, what a sixth song!

Alvin Lee introduced the band's final number with, "This is a thing called I'm going home...by helicopter." By helicopter? Long story! The guitarist ripped into his heavily stickered red Gibson ES-335 (nicknamed Big Red), spewing out notes like a Gatling gun. His bandmates tore into a blues-boogie progression that sped along at breakneck speed.

While the cameras locked onto Alvin Lee, they also captured Leo Lyon's spasmodic head jerks. Keyboardist Chick Churchill had a few of his own head-banging moments. For many, "I'm Going Home" was the highlight of the Woodstock film, and it hoisted Alvin and the band to star status.

> **ALVIN LEE:** We found [the film] took our music a little out of context. We became celluloid figures. [Younger fans] were coming to our concerts and not really listening. They were just shouting for "I'm Going Home."

Following their Woodstock performance, TYA toured the United States endlessly and played nearly every major city while packing the biggest venues. And like Cream before them, TYA's concert songs extended well

Alvin Lee.

beyond their recorded times. The quartet that built its following as an underground band playing small clubs had now lost that personal connection with its audience.

> RIC LEE: Alvin always called us an underground band. We really and truly were a blues band, but Alvin considered us progressive. When you listen to our music, we never played straight blues. We always twisted it a bit.

TYA will be remembered for their amalgam of blues, jazz, rock 'n' roll and rockabilly and a bit of psychedelic rock typical of the times. At times, they were loud and raucous. Other times, they maintained the class and sophistication of a small jazz combo at an intimate lounge. There was a real chemistry that served the band well for many years.

MUSICAL INFLUENCES WHO MATTER

Elvis Presley, Johnny Cash, Lonnie Donegan, Roy Orbison, Eddie Cochran, "Brother" Jack McDuff, Jimmy Smith, Thelonious Monk, Carl Perkins, Beethoven, Chuck Berry, Little Richard, Jerry Lee Lewis, Scotty Moore, Jack Bruce, Ginger Baker, Etta James, Pinetop Smith, John Lee Hooker, Muddy Waters, Howlin' Wolf, Big Bill Broonzy, Lonnie Johnson, Sonny Boy Williamson, Leadbelly, Steve Miller, Charlie Christian, Chet Atkins, Django Reinhart, George Benson, Wes Montgomery, Eric Clapton, Jimi Hendrix, Albert Lee.

PROBABLE CONCERT SETLIST:
INTERNATIONAL AMPHITHEATER, AUGUST 17, 1975

"Rock 'n' Roll Music to the World," "Love Like a Man," "Good Morning Little School Girl," "Slow Blues in C," "Hobbit," "One of These Days," "Classical Thing," "Scat Thing," "Lord I Just Can't Keep from Crying," "I'm Going Home," "Sweet Little Sixteen," "Choo Choo Mama."

HUMBLE PIE

FORMED 1969

BAND MEMBERS WHO MATTER

Steve Marriott (guitar, vocals, harmonica, keyboards), Peter Frampton (guitar, vocals, keyboards), Greg Ridley (bass, guitar, vocals), Jerry Shirley (drums, percussion, keyboards), Dave "Clem" Clempson (guitar, vocals, keyboards).

> JERRY SHIRLEY: As for live performing and working a stage and audience, [Steve] helped invent a lot of what is taken for granted in rock 'n' roll performance today.

WHY THEY MATTER

For a brief time, British band Humble Pie was one of the biggest draws in America along with the Rolling Stones, Pink Floyd, the Who and Led Zeppelin. Although lacking hit singles, they connected with American audiences through several key albums and sweaty, swaggering live performances.

The recipe for Humble Pie was simple: fill a large concert venue with frenzied fans; mix in ample amounts of high-energy rock, boogie and blues; and let the ingredients bake at high heat for about two hours.

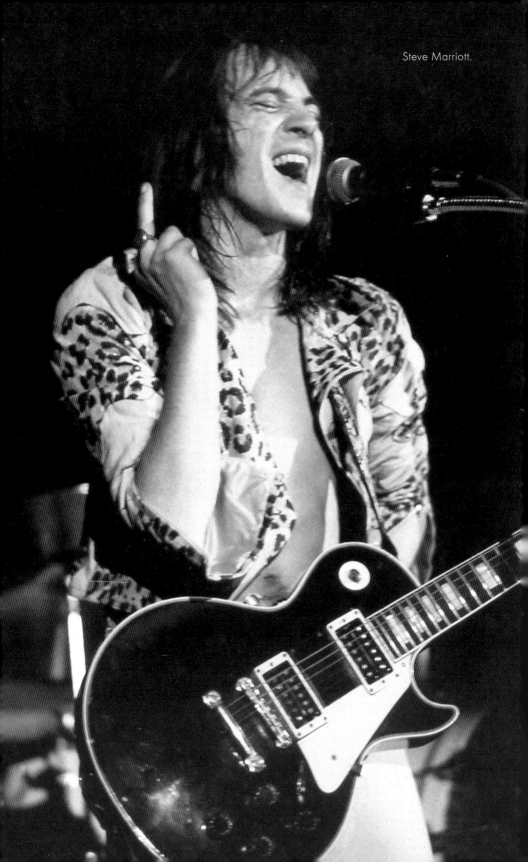
Steve Marriott.

PETER FRAMPTON: For me, the great thing about Humble Pie was that we [represented] energy unlimited. We were all at the age where we were just going for it.

Despite the band's musically raucous reputation, early Pie was at home writing and playing melodic ballads and unplugged music. Their early music benefited from a more balanced approach and Peter Frampton's influence. His potent but understated guitar style and pleasant singing voice were the perfect counterbalance to Marriott's tendency toward overstatement. Ironically, it was Marriott who insisted that the band include an acoustic set in their early concerts.

The band took shape in late 1968 when Marriott departed the Small Faces. He placed a call to "teen scream" guitarist Peter Frampton (the Herd) to form a new band with Greg Ridley on bass and Jerry Shirley on drums. Expectations and hype ran high in the British press.

The diminutive Marriott possessed an upper register singing voice of incredible power and resonance. And while high-energy rock was his strength, he was at home with soul and blues standards, ballads and even country western–flavored tunes.

PAUL STANLEY: He had a great voice. He was one of my heroes. I saw Marriott live with Humble Pie and it was like being at a church revival, and that is the coolest thing you can do, turn your performance into an evangelical event.

Following critical reviews and financial issues, Pie retooled. New management pushed Marriott to the forefront and refocused the band's sound on the hard rock, blues and boogie that American audiences craved.

STEVE MARRIOTT: The music's got more guts now and our writing is derived more from the Muddy Waters and Willie Dixon school. The acoustic stuff didn't work unless the audience was quiet, and I think it's embarrassing and pretentious to ask an audience to be quiet. People want to see you work yourself into a sweat.

In 1971, the band with so much promise was rewarded. The studio album *Rock On* had been their most successful LP to date and marked a turning point. It also hinted at Marriott's desire to reach into soul and gospel with singing credits given to Doris Troy and Claudia Lennear,

Steve Marriott (*left*) and Clem Clempson.

whose résumés included Pink Floyd, the Rolling Stones, Joe Cocker and George Harrison.

Later that year, Pie released a live album that captured the type of performance that turned on American audiences. *Performance: Rockin' the Fillmore* showcased the band's heavy-metal blues crunch, but it also marked the end of the Peter Frampton era. The guitarist went on to become one of the biggest rock stars of the 1970s.

Frampton was immediately replaced by talented axman Dave "Clem" Clempson, whose Eric Clapton–style guitar work meshed well with Pie's hardened sound. The result was *Smokin'*, the band's most commercially successful studio album.

With Pie's growing popularity, Marriott felt comfortable indulging his longtime passion for gospel, soul and rhythm 'n' blues. But with their best years in the rearview mirror, Humble Pie disbanded in 1975 before a final resurrection in 1980.

MUSICAL INFLUENCES WHO MATTER

Buddy Holly, Ray Charles, Otis Redding, James Brown, Rufus Thomas, Booker T. & the M.G.'s, Muddy Waters, Willie Dixon, Bobby "Blue" Bland, Charles Mingus, Eddie Cochran, Hank Marvin, the Beatles, Gene Krupa, Buddy Rich, Keith Moon, Mitch Mitchell, Charlie Watts.

PROBABLE CONCERT SETLIST: INTERNATIONAL AMPHITHEATER, DECEMBER 9, 1973

"Honky Tonk Women," "Oh La De Da," "Hallelujah I Love Her So," "I Believe to My Soul," "I Don't Need No Doctor," "30 Days in the Hole," "Hot 'n' Nasty," "I'm Ready," "Strange Days."

Peter Frampton.

PETER FRAMPTON

GUITAR, SINGER, SONGWRITER, BANDLEADER

PETER FRAMPTON: It was fun for a while until I realized that it didn't matter whether I came on with or without a guitar. It was going to be the same reaction and they weren't listening.

WHY HE MATTERS

During his teen years with the British band the Herd, Peter Frampton's boyish good looks and curly blond mane helped make him a star. Unfortunately, it was this superficial celebrity that delayed Frampton's acceptance as a formidable guitar player and serious musician.

He recognized the need to shed this image reinforced by the British press and legions of screaming British teenage girls. In 1969, he responded by forming the rock band Humble Pie with former Small Faces guitarist and singer Steve Marriott.

While Steve Marriott worshipped at the altar of Muddy Waters, Frampton envisioned himself more a Kenny Burrell and Wes Montgomery type of guitar player. In 1971, Frampton left Humble Pie.

By the mid-1970s, it had paid off. After achieving some commercial success with his fourth solo album, *Frampton*, he hit the road with Bob Mayo on backing vocals, guitar and keyboards; Stanley Sheldon on vocals and bass; and John Siomos on drums. With his band in top form, Frampton released a double live LP covering several concerts at San Francisco's famed Winterland venue.

The resulting *Frampton Comes Alive* was a landmark release that sold more than sixteen million copies internationally and spawned three hit singles: "Show Me the Way," "Baby I Love Your Way" and "Do You Feel Like We Do." Frampton had now received the recognition he long desired. Steven Ford, President Gerald Ford's music-loving son, invited the British axman to the White House. Now that's recognition!

Frampton followed with *I'm in You*, a successful album that peaked at no. 2 and yielded two hit singles. Over the next two decades, Frampton recorded, toured and found additional opportunities in television, advertising and movies.

The new millennium brought Frampton renewed recognition and success. In 2004, he became an American citizen—a land where he felt his music was better appreciated. In 2006, he received a Grammy award for his innovative instrumental album *Fingerprints*.

PETER FRAMPTON: Awards aren't supposed to enhance one's creative juices, but they don't hurt. With the Grammy, I feel validated as the musician that I always felt I've been.

His 2010 release, *Thank You Mr. Churchill*, demonstrated his hard rock credentials, and in 2019, he devoted an album to his favorite blues music classics.

For those who've followed Frampton's six-decade career, there has never been any doubt about his musical abilities. As for Frampton, he remarked, "It took so long for me to realize that success isn't measured in how many albums you sell or how many concert tickets people buy, but rather by an internal barometer. I've realized that success isn't what you think…but what I think."

Despite a degenerative muscle disease that necessitated a seated performance, Frampton felt fit enough to schedule a 2024 tour titled Never Say Never. He noted, "I'm just a glutton for enjoyment."

MUSICAL INFLUENCES WHO MATTER

Motown, Funk Brothers, Django Reinhardt, Charlie Christian, Kenny Burrell, Wes Montgomery, Cliff Richards & the Shadows, Hank Marvin, Eddie Cochran, the Ventures, Jimi Hendrix, the Beatles, Eric Clapton, Jeff Beck, Jimmy Smith.

PROBABLE CONCERT SETLIST:
AUDITORIUM THEATRE, JUNE 23, 1974

"It's a Plain Shame," "Doobie Wah," "Lines on My Face," "The Lodger," "I Wanna Go to the Sun," "Do You Feel Like We Do," "Jumpin' Jack Flash," "White Sugar," "Shine On."

GOLDEN EARRING

FORMED 1961

BAND MEMBERS WHO MATTER

George Kooymans (guitar, vocals), Rinus Gerritsen (bass, keyboards), Barry Hay (guitar, vocals, flute, saxophone), Cesar Zuiderwijk (drums, percussion).

> **GEORGE KOOYMANS:** You can't keep playing in Holland....People invest money in bands, but the Dutch don't. It's very risky because it's not possible to sell a lot of records. The only time they did was with the band Focus.

WHY THEY MATTER

Longevity in the rock 'n' roll business is precarious, and the year 2021 dealt a blow for two bands with the longest-running intact lineups. In the case of ZZ Top, it was the passing of bassist Dusty Hill. For Golden Earring, it was a career-ending health diagnosis for founding member George Kooymans.

Before Golden Earring cracked the American market, the boys from the Netherlands were stars in their homeland. Stardom in the United States was more elusive and confined to their hits "Radar Love" (1973), "Twilight Zone" (1982) and "Quiet Eyes" (1986). The albums *Moontan* (1973) and *Cut* (1982) were the only two that sold well enough to crack Billboard's Hot 100 chart.

George Kooymans.

But their fleeting success in the U.S. market came not from lack of effort. From 1969 through 1984, they toured the country thirteen times and shared the stage with the Who, Eric Clapton, Santana, the Doobie Brothers, Led Zeppelin, Kiss, Aerosmith, Rush and Lynyrd Skynyrd.

With the band's classic lineup in place, the 1970s marked a period of growth as the band began adding stage theatrics and better sound and lighting thanks to their relationship with the Who. In 1972, they toured with the Who and signed with the band's record company.

BARRY HAY: This was our single most important move. Somebody started believing in us. [The Who] saw something nobody else saw.

Golden Earring's persistence paid off with the 1973 release of *Moontan* and one of rock music's all-time great driving songs, "Radar Love." The song was later used to wake up a space shuttle crew and the Mars explorer vehicle.

BARRY HAY: I was brainstorming [with friends]....The idea of an ordinary guy in his car took shape and when my American house guest returned home and read the lyrics, he went wild and said, "This is brilliant...the ultimate American car song!"

With "Radar Love," the boyhood dreams of band founders Gerritsen and Kooymans were coming true. But from a Dutch point of view, they found the American music industry fixated on formats and band categorizations. As a result, Golden Earring gave their management fits.

As pressure for a follow-up hit grew, the quartet added a keyboard player and horns to avoid making a clone of "Radar Love." This sound shift confused U.S. fans and the international press. In 1984, MTV helped Golden Earring recapture American audiences with the hard-rocking song "Twilight Zone" and the album *Cut*. But the momentum was short-lived, and with mounting financial difficulties, they played their last U.S. concert in 1984.

The band continued to make records and tour Europe, but in 2021, guitarist George Kooymans was diagnosed with ALS and their incredible ride was over. Barry Hay remarked, "This is a death blow. We always said we would keep going until one of us fell over. I didn't expect George to be the first. Kooymans was always the toughest of the four of us."

MUSICAL INFLUENCES WHO MATTER

Little Richard, Lloyd Price, Fats Domino, Elvis Presley, the Yardbirds, Gerry and the Pacemakers, the Beatles, the Byrds, the Rolling Stones, Cream, Led Zeppelin, Pink Floyd.

PROBABLE CONCERT SETLIST: AUDITORIUM THEATRE, OCTOBER 30, 1974

"She Flies on Strange Wings," "Big Tree Blue Sea," "Candy's Going Bad," "Radar Love," "I Can't Get a Hold on Her," "I'm Going to Send My Pigeons to the Sky."

Joe Walsh.

JOE WALSH / BARNSTORM

GUITAR, SINGER, SONGWRITER, BANDLEADER, KEYBOARDS

JOE WALSH: I'd just like to be a creative spokesman for my generation and to go down as being valid. If I can do that and make some people happy with the music, it's well worth all the brain cells it took me to do it.

WHY HE MATTERS

This seven-decade American rock icon often gets lost when "greatest musician" lists are compiled. Although Joe Walsh has referred to himself as a third-generation blues student, it was Pete Townshend's trademark rhythm/lead technique that heavily influenced the musician during a 1970 James Gang tour with the Who.

Walsh's guitar work can be breathtaking: an amalgam of hard rock, country rock, funk and blues. His slide guitar technique and tone evoke memories of the late Duane Allman.

Although not blessed with a conventionally pleasing singing voice, his vocals sound refreshingly imperfect and have served his music well. He has endeared himself to legions through his sense of humor, charm and down-to-earth demeanor.

Joe Fidler Walsh was born in Wichita, Kansas, on November 20, 1947. After moving to Ohio, Joe majored in English and minored in music at Kent State University. On May 4, 1970, the National Guard fired on campus demonstrators, killing four and wounding nine students. It changed his life.

JOE WALSH: After that, I didn't look at college the same. The James Gang started to gather momentum, and I decided I'd try pursuing music as a profession. I decided that maybe I don't need a degree that bad.

By the time he joined the James Gang, he was a potent guitarist, songwriter and vocalist. After three studio albums, he found the band musically confining. He formed the band Barnstorm with multi-instrumentalist Kenny Passarelli and drummer Joe Vitale.

Barnstorm made one self-titled album before Passarelli and Vitale backed Walsh on two additional albums. To this day, the song "Rocky Mountain Way" still receives heavy airplay and is considered a rock classic.

JOE WALSH: One day I was in my backyard in Boulder [Colorado] mowing the lawn and I was thinking, "Boy, I sure hope leaving the James Gang was a good idea!" And then I looked up...and there were the Rocky Mountains. It just hit me how beautiful it all was five thousand feet up. And that was it—the words came.

In 1976, Walsh made a game-changing move. He replaced Bernie Leadon in the Eagles and brought his muscular rhythm work and hot guitar riffs to the band's country rock sound. With Walsh on board, the Eagles experienced a massive resurgence supported by several blockbuster albums, hit songs and tours. But despite enormous success, the excesses of a rock 'n' roll lifestyle took a toll on Walsh. His song "Life's Been Good" from his solo album *But Seriously Folks* is an ode to rock star money, indulgences and bad behavior.

Although the Eagles officially disbanded in 1980, they've reunited, toured and recorded several times with Walsh and new members. Tangential to his time with the Eagles, Walsh recorded solo albums, contributed to movie soundtracks, played with other heavyweight rock artists and frequently appeared as a guest on television and radio programs. He's contributed time and money to a variety of humanitarian causes.

MUSICAL INFLUENCES WHO MATTER

Les Paul, Eddie Cochran, Carl Perkins, Bill Haley, James Burton, Elvis Presley, the Beach Boys, Chuck Berry, the Beatles, Pete Townshend, Jeff Beck, Eric Clapton, Jimmy Page, Mike Bloomfield, Albert Collins, B.B. King, Freddie King, Albert King, the Ronettes, Motown.

PROBABLE CONCERT SETLIST: JOE WALSH AND BARNSTORM, AUDITORIUM THEATRE, NOVEMBER 5, 1973

"Here We Go," "Midnight Visitor," "One and One," "Giant Bohemoth," "Mother Says," "Birdcall Morning," "Home," "I'll Tell the World About You," "Turn to Stone," "Comin' Down," "Rocky Mountain Way."

J. GEILS BAND

FORMED 1967

BAND MEMBERS WHO MATTER

J. Geils (guitar), Peter Wolf (lead vocals), Dick "Magic Dick" Salwitz (harmonica, saxophone, trumpet), Danny Klein (bass), Seth Justman (keyboards, vocals), Stephan Jo Bladd (drums, vocals).

WHY THEY MATTER

During the 1960s, rock concerts were rarely authorized in culturally conservative Boston. So, music executives hatched a marketing plan to develop local bands as the city's response to San Francisco's music scene. The J. Geils Band balked at this scheme.

In retrospect, the band's decision to pursue its own musical principles was a wise one. Times changed, and the Boston area became known for several legendary rock acts like Aerosmith, Boston and the J. Geils Band. The latter made some of the most danceable and honest rock music of the era. The original lineup remained intact for nearly fifteen years, with thirteen albums and a slew of memorable songs.

To those outside of New England, the band was best known for its early 1980s hits "Love Stinks," "Freeze-Frame" and "Centerfold." But for hometown fans, they were always the local bad boys who rocked Boston venues a decade earlier. Their funky brand of blues rock and sweaty party

J. Geils.

anthems included "First I Look at the Purse," "Whammer Jammer," "Homework," "It Ain't Nothin' (But a House Party)," "Must of Got Lost," "Looking for Love" and "I Don't Need You No More."

Their road to stardom began in 1968 when an Atlantic Records promotion man was visiting Boston and overheard what he thought was a southside Chicago blues band. To his surprise, he found five Caucasian musicians. Shortly thereafter, they were signed by Atlantic Records—home to many rhythm 'n' blues legends.

> **PETER WOLF:** We were tickled pink man. We thought we'd end up on Ding-Dang records or something like that. The first time we met all those guys from Atlantic, we asked them about Wilson Pickett and Don Covay. Atlantic was like some kind of dream because of the catalogue they had.

Although guitarist J. Geils was the band's namesake, frontman Peter Wolf grabbed the most attention in concert. His stage presence was a cross between a Mick Jagger, soul men Sam and Dave, a mobster and a vaudeville entertainer. Another riveting stage figure and standout musician was Dick Salwitz (aka Magic Dick). With a massive black Afro, dark shades and an almost obscene instrumental virtuosity, he was referred to as the Jimi Hendrix of the blues harp.

> **DICK SALWITZ:** When I was three years old, I had a pretty bad case of the flu. My mother bought me a Marine Band harmonica. I'd blow into it, and the sound that came out, and how it felt in [my] hand made a big impression on me. There was something magical about it.

The J. Geils Band was a unit greater than its parts and rarely placed virtuosity above song. Throughout the 1970s, they toured endlessly and stayed afloat thanks to a large word-of-mouth following and critically acclaimed performances. Their live shows were legendary.

In 1983, Wolf took his songs and began a solo career. Keyboardist Seth Justman assumed lead vocals and creative control until 1985, when the unit called it quits and came together for a few one-off gigs.

Peter Wolf.

MUSICAL INFLUENCES WHO MATTER

Chicago blues, early Motown, the Stax-Volt-Memphis sound, doo wop, bebop, rhythm 'n' blues, swing, big band jazz.

PROBABLE CONCERT SETLIST:
AUDITORIUM THEATRE, MARCH 26, 1975

"Did You No Wrong," "Southside Shuffle," "Gettin' Out," "Givin' It All Up," "Must of Got Lost," "Detroit Breakdown," "Lookin' for a Love," "Chimes," "Whammer Jammer," "Ain't Nothin' But a House Party," "I Would Hate to See You Go," "Give It to Me," "First I Look at the Purse."

MONTROSE

FORMED 1973

BAND MEMBERS WHO MATTER

Ronnie Montrose (guitar), Sammy Hagar (lead vocals), Bill Church (bass), Denny Carmassi (drums), Alan Fitzgerald (bass).

> RONNIE MONTROSE: What I do isn't dictated by what audiences like. If it happens to be appreciated, great! If it gets to where you're doin' what somebody's tellin' you to do—then it's just a [crappy] job and I'll go back to working in a gas station.

WHY THEY MATTER

Occasionally, a rock band comes along that leaves a mark greater than its commercial success or longevity. In 1973, four musicians and a creative sound engineer made an album that pulled the sound of 1960s British blues rock closer to the sound of metal and "hair" bands that emerged in the late 1970s and 1980s. That band was Montrose.

Ronnie Montrose—the band's namesake—had previously worked with the Edgar Winter Group ("Free Ride," "Frankenstein") and backed other notables such Herbie Hancock, Tony Williams, Boz Scaggs, Gary Wright, the Neville Brothers and Van Morrison (on Van's album *Tupelo Honey*).

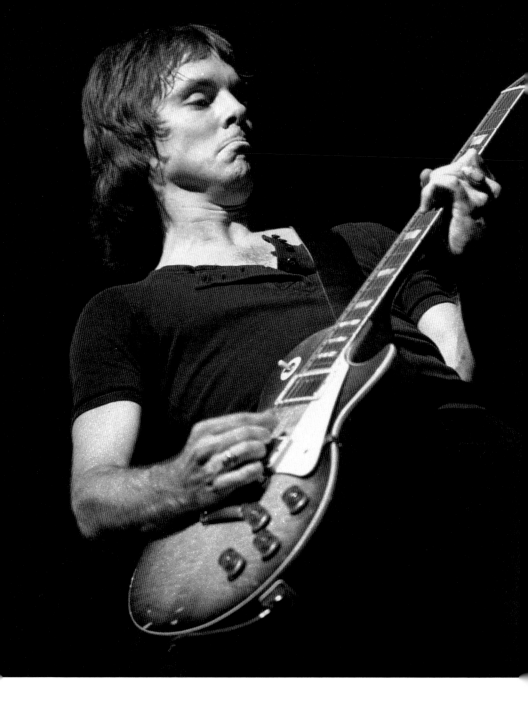

The debut album *Montrose* received only token support from Warner Brothers and stalled at no. 133 on the Billboard 200 chart. Nevertheless, the LP produced several crotch-rocking anthems that ushered in a new wave of American hard rock. Among these were "Rock Candy," "I Got the

Opposite:
Ronnie
Montrose.

Right:
Sammy Hagar.

Fire," "Bad Motor Scooter," "Make It Last," "Rock the Nation" and "Space Station #5." These songs showcased the bone-crushing guitar tone of Ronnie Montrose and the upper register vocal shredding of the charismatic Sammy Hagar.

SAMMY HAGAR: Ronnie Montrose gave me my first break as a songwriter, as a front man, as a recording artist, and as a touring artist...and for that I will always be grateful.

Subsequent albums charted higher, but few equaled the swagger of the band's debut effort.

RONNIE MONTROSE: Montrose was never the same after Sammy and Bill Church left. The dynamic of the original band was singular and powerful.

Following the departure of Hagar and Church, Ronnie continued to tour and record as Montrose, launched a solo career, formed the trailblazing band Gamma and appeared as a guest guitarist. Prior to his untimely death in 2012, Ronnie had begun laying down tracks for an ambitious project that would feature ten songs with ten different vocalists. The album *10 x 10*—released in 2017—was completed with the assistance of several renowned guest musicians and brims with inspired musicianship.

Sammy Hagar went solo and produced several rock classics before famously replacing David Lee Roth in Van Halen.

MUSICAL INFLUENCES WHO MATTER

The Yardbirds, Jeff Beck Group, Jimmy Page and Led Zeppelin, Cream, Faces, Jimi Hendrix, Johnny Winter, James Dewar (Robin Trower's band), MC5, the Who, Deep Purple, Cactus, the McCoys, Steppenwolf.

PROBABLE CONCERT SETLIST:
AUDITORIUM THEATRE, JUNE 23, 1974

"Good Rocking Tonight," "Bad Motor Scooter," "Make It Last," "How Many More Years," "Rock the Nation," "Space Station #5," "Roll Over Beethoven," "Rock Candy."

BAD COMPANY

FORMED 1973

BAND MEMBERS WHO MATTER

Paul Rodgers (lead vocals, keyboards, guitar and harmonica), Mick Ralphs (lead guitar, keyboards), Boz Burrell (bass and vocals), Simon Kirke (drums and vocals).

> MICK RALPHS: Well, I think we should be in there [The Rock & Roll Hall of Fame]. It would be a nice accomplishment. I don't really know how they go about the vetting process. If you'd like, put in a good word for me!

WHY THEY MATTER

In the late 1960s, the music press coined the term *supergroup*. This designation created excessive hype and unrealistic expectations that sank bands like Blind Faith. The label had no effect on Bad Company, one of the most popular and commercially successful British rock bands of the 1970s.

Singer Paul Rodgers and drummer Simon Kirke had previously earned their rock creds in the British band Free. Rodgers's virile and soulful voice would inspire Freddie Mercury (Queen) and Ronnie Van Zant (Lynyrd Skynyrd).

Paul Rodgers.

Rodgers then met guitarist and songwriter Mick Ralphs—a member of the successful British glam band Mott the Hoople. Ralphs had songs that Mott frontman Ian Hunter couldn't or wouldn't sing.

The final slot in Bad Company's original lineup was filled by King Crimson bassist Raymond "Boz" Burrell, a singer who first learned bass guitar from King Crimson guitarist Robert Fripp.

With the new quartet managed by Led Zeppelin's manager Peter Grant, Bad Company made five studio albums in five years and toured endlessly to packed arenas worldwide.

> **PAUL RODGERS:** We tried to manage ourselves with Free, and that didn't work, so I approached Peter Grant [for] Bad Company. I called him up and it was sort of like calling up God.

On the studio side, the band released three consecutive million-plus-selling albums that spawned an army of rock radio staples. The five-time platinum *Bad Company* was known for "Can't Get Enough," "Rock Steady," "Ready for Love," "Bad Company" and "Movin' On." The three-time platinum *Straight Shooter* had its share of memorable songs like "Good Lovin' Gone Bad," "Feel Like Makin' Love" and "Shooting Star." And last was *Run with the Pack*, which generated radio favorites "Run with the Pack" and "Silver, Blue and Gold."

More albums followed in 1977 and 1979. *Burnin' Sky* and *Desolation Angels* climbed high up the U.S. and U.K. charts and contained radio favorites "Burnin' Sky" and "Rock 'n' Roll Fantasy."

In 1982, Paul Rodgers walked away following the release of *Rough Diamonds*. Mick Ralphs—an English country boy at heart—said the timing was right for all to take a much-needed break.

Four years later, Bad Company began a new era. From 1986 through 1994, Mick Ralphs and Simon Kirke recorded and toured under the Bad Company name with permission from Rodgers, who later regretted his decision.

In 1999, a long-awaited reunion of the original members produced several successful singles from the critically acclaimed CD *The Original Bad Company Anthology*. A successful U.S. tour preceded the album's release, but the reunion was short-lived.

Mick Ralphs "retired" from touring, and Boz Burrell worked with John Lord, Alvin Lee and others before suffering a fatal heart attack in September 2006.

Opposite: Mick Ralphs. *Above, left to right:* Boz Burrell, Paul Rodgers, Simon Kirke and Mick Ralphs.

In 2010, Rodgers, Ralphs and Kirke reunited for a well-received tour of Great Britain, North America and Japan. They were joined by guitarist Howard Leese (ex-Heart) and bassist Lynn Sorenson. In 2016, Mick Ralphs suffered a serious stroke and focused on his rehabilitation. As of this writing, Rodgers and Kirke remain active in music.

MUSICAL INFLUENCES WHO MATTER

Led Zeppelin, Cream, Jimi Hendrix, the Beatles, Buffalo Springfield, Otis Redding, Steve Cropper, Booker T. & the M.G.'s, Albert King, Freddie King, B.B. King, James Burton, Leslie West.

PROBABLE CONCERT SETLIST:
CHICAGO STADIUM, APRIL 23, 1976

"Live for the Music," "Good Lovin' Gone Bad," "Simple Man," "Young Blood," "Wild Fire Woman," "Feel Like Makin' Love," "Deal with the Preacher," "Ready for Love," "Sweet Lil' Sister," "Shooting Star," "Silver, Blue & Gold, "Run with the Pack," "Rock Steady," "Honey Child," "Can't Get Enough."

Jimmy Page.

LED ZEPPELIN

FORMED 1968

BAND MEMBERS WHO MATTER

Jimmy Page (guitars, backing vocals, producer), Robert Plant (lead vocals, harmonica), John Paul Jones (bass, keyboards, mandolin, backing vocals, arranger), John Bonham (drums, percussion, backing vocals).

ROBERT PLANT: Zeppelin was the greatest adventure of my life.

WHY THEY MATTER

Jimmy Page, Robert Plant, John Paul Jones and John "Bonzo" Bonham put the "heavy" into blues rock. The quartet applied a modern rock approach to Mississippi Delta blues, British folk and world music. On vinyl, they put down some of rock music's most monolithic riffs with songs like "Whole Lotta Love," "Dazed and Confused," "Communication Breakdown," "Good Times Bad Times," "Kashmir," "Immigrant Song," "Black Dog" and "Misty Mountain Hop."

They built their sound around Page's riffs (some conceived by Jones), Plant's orgasmic blues wails and a "shock and awe" rhythm section (Bonham and Jones) that knew how to swing.

But unlike many bands they spawned, Zeppelin understood finesse and crescendo. They valued cross-influences to build songs that spanned the dynamic range. As former session players, Jones and Page understood how to use the recording studio to their advantage.

> **JOHN PAUL JONES:** [We] weren't a purist band. Between the blues influences of Robert and the rock 'n' roll influences of Jimmy who also had strong blues influences; the soul influences of "Bonzo"; and my soul and jazz influences, there seemed to be a common area which was Led Zeppelin. It was the fusion of different types of music and interests.

Yet from the beginning, Zeppelin was reviled by segments of the music press.

> **JIMMY PAGE:** There was a certain amount of acid poured on us. I saw it as venomous [back] then. I'll give the reviewers the benefit of the doubt as each album was so different from the other. After [our first two albums], you get Led Zeppelin III. Acoustic guitars? What's this about? There were crazy conclusions, but it made me more determined.

On stage, Zeppelin had few peers. They were improvisational giants and model rock gods who broke box office records in the mid-1970s. Their prowess as musicians was matched only by their reputation (some of it farfetched) for debauchery.

The seeds of Zeppelin began with Jimmy Page. As a member of the Yardbirds, he was planning his next move that would build on the success of Cream and the original Jeff Beck Group. First on board was John Paul Jones, a multi-instrumentalist whom Page first met during session work. Like Page, Jones was a prolific studio musician, director and arranger who had contributed his skills to many of the era's pop stars.

> **JIMMY PAGE:** [John Paul Jones] didn't need me for a job. He is unquestionably an incredible arranger and musician. It was just that he felt the need to express himself and thought we might be able to do it together. I jumped at the chance of getting him.

When Page's first choices for a singer and drummer were unavailable, he was pointed in the direction of Robert Plant, who in turn recommended John Bonham. According to Page, the quartet rehearsed in a small room and jammed on "Train Kept a-Rollin," a rockabilly tune popularized by the Yardbirds. The chemistry was there.

Robert Plant.

When the Yardbirds disbanded in 1968, Page, Plant, Jones and Bonham fulfilled previously booked engagements under the name "New Yardbirds" before entering the studio to complete Led Zeppelin's self-titled debut album. They played their first North American show in Denver on the day after Christmas 1968.

Left to right: Robert Plant, Jimmy Page and John Paul Jones.

John Bonham.

Released in early 1969, *Led Zeppelin I* marked a momentous turn in the evolution of hard rock. Powerful proto-punk speed rockers like "Communication Breakdown" influenced future punk guitarists like Johnny Ramone. "Dazed and Confused"—a song probing the depths of despair—contrasted sharply with delicate folk tunes like "Black Mountain Side." The boys also paid homage to their blues idols with versions of "You Shook Me" and "I Can't Quit You Baby."

Led Zeppelin II was recorded during a frenzied touring schedule and released in October 1969. It knocked *Abbey Road* from the top of the charts and remained there for seven weeks. "Whole Lotta Love" ushered in a new era of blues-metal barnstormers while songs like "Thank You," "Ramble On," "Bring It on Home" and "What Is and Should Never Be," demonstrated Zeppelin's ability to incorporate tempo changes and dynamics.

Led Zeppelin III placed greater emphasis on Zeppelin's interest in mythology and music derived from folk, Celtic and country influences along with the use of acoustic guitars to create texture.

Their magnum opus arrived in November 1971 with *Led Zeppelin IV* and epic rock anthems like "Stairway to Heaven." The band's musical diversity and muscle on that recording still inspire awe.

Left to right: Robert Plant, Jimmy Page and John Paul Jones.

Over the next two years, Zeppelin continued their foray into musical experimentation that included funk and reggae. Their fifth album—*Houses of the Holy*—was released in the spring of 1973. It was the first Zeppelin album title not referencing the band's name. The title was a metaphor for the sacred concert venues where fans flocked. Two years later, the quartet followed up with the charts-topping double LP *Physical Graffiti*. It was the band's first on their own record label (Swan Song) and featured a half-dozen Zeppelin classics, including "Kasmir" and "The Rover." The band threw fans a curveball with the song "Boogie with Stu" featuring Stones pianist Ian Stewart doing what he did best.

Zeppelin was now the most popular band in the world in terms of record sales and box office receipts. They were flying around in a leased jet emblazoned with the Led Zeppelin font.

In 1976, Zeppelin released the concert film *The Song Remains the Same*, capturing 1973 shows at Madison Square Garden. However, a far better document of Zeppelin in concert is the triple LP *How the West Was Won*. Released in 2003 and taken from two Los Angeles concerts in 1972, it represents Zeppelin at the peak of their powers.

In Through the Out Door—the quartet's final original material album—was released in mid-1979 and topped the U.S. and British charts. Tragedy struck the following year. While preparing their first North American tour since 1977, drummer John Bonham was found dead in the Windsor home of Jimmy Page, where the band was rehearsing. It was a devasting blow.

JOHN PAUL JONES: [John Bonham and I] were both huge Motown and Stax fans which is one reason I've always said that Zeppelin was one of the few bands to "swing." We actually had a groove in those days. People used to come to our shows and dance. You didn't necessarily see that at a Black Sabbath show or whatever.

On December 4, 1980, the remaining members and manager released a simple press statement: "[Circumstances] led us to decide that we could not continue as we were." Surviving members moved on to other music projects and on special occasions reunited with Jason Bonham taking his father's spot behind the drum kit.

Led Zeppelin remains historic—a bigger-than-life band in the world of rock 'n' roll. Their name is held in the highest regard for artistic achievement, commercial success and ongoing influence. They were inducted into the Rock & Roll Hall of Fame in 1995.

MUSICAL INFLUENCES WHO MATTER

Howlin' Wolf, Willie Dixon, Albert King, Otis Rush, Sonny Boy Williamson, Robert Johnson, Bukka White, Elmore James, Sleepy John Estes, John Lee Hooker, Skip James, B.B. King, Freddie King, Hubert Sumlin, Phil Upchurch, Fats Domino, James Brown, Elvis Presley, Joni Mitchell, Fairport Convention, Scotty Moore, James Burton, Bert Jansch, Frank Zappa, the Byrds, Santana, Jefferson Airplane, Umm Kulthum, Charlie Mingus, Ray Brown, Scott LaFaro, Gene Krupa, Buddy Rich, Ginger Baker, Art Blakey, Max Roach, Louis Bellson, the Graham Bond Organization.

PROBABLE CONCERT SETLIST:
CHICAGO STADIUM, APRIL 10, 1977

"The Song Remains the Same," "Sick Again," "Nobody's Fault but Mine," "In My Time of Dying," "Since I've Been Loving You," "No Quarter," "Ten Years Gone," "The Battle of Evermore," "Going to California," "Black Country Woman," "Bron-Y-Aur Stomp," "Trampled Under Foot," "White Summer," "Black Mountain Side," "Kashmir," "Moby Dick," "Achilles Last Stand," "Stairway to Heaven," "Rock and Roll."

JEFF BECK

GUITAR, SONGWRITER, COMPOSER, BANDLEADER

JEFF BECK: There were times when I treated my guitars as a nuisance. I looked at one the other day and thought, "Thanks a lot, pal, you got me all around the world."

WHY HE MATTERS

Geoffrey Arnold "Jeff" Beck was born on June 24, 1944, in Wallington, Surrey, England. He was initially inspired by the music that comforted his parents during World War II. He described his first guitar as a lump of wood with some wires—humble beginnings for a man whose peers have used more than a few superlatives to describe his musicianship.

Over his seven-decade career, the age-defying guitarist explored psychedelia, blues, rock, pop, fusion, metal, funk, rockabilly, classical, opera and electronica. Musically, he never stood still. Beck accumulated eight Grammy awards and was twice inducted (as a Yardbird and solo artist) into the Rock & Roll Hall of Fame.

In a 1975 interview with *Guitar Player* magazine, the ever-modest Beck explained, "I like to play easy things that sound hard." What Beck did was play hard things and make them look easy. Despite Beck's career, in which commercial success lagged behind other guitar legends, a *New York Times* writer called him "the greatest guitarist that millions of people have never heard of."

Jeff Beck.

JEFF BECK: It's a diabolical business. I can't imagine how hellish it must be to be hounded like Amy Winehouse and people like that. I have a little peripheral place on the outskirts of celebrity when I go to premieres and that sort of stuff...which is as close as I want to get.

Whether the industrial crunch of an album like *Jeff Beck's Guitar Shop* or a delicate passage played for a Luciano Pavarotti recording, few guitarists could make an electric guitar howl like Godzilla and then trill like a songbird. As *Musician* magazine noted, he beat Hendrix to feedback and fuzz and Eddie Van Halen to finger tapping.

At age twenty, Beck's recording career began with rock 'n' roll eccentric Screaming Lord Sutch. In 1965, he replaced Eric Clapton in the Yardbirds. With Beck in the band, the Yardbirds racked up four Top 20 Billboard singles: "I'm a Man," "Heart Full of Soul," "Over Under Sideways Down" and "Shapes of Things." Jimmy Page joined the band, and for several months, he and Beck shared guitar duties before Beck was unceremoniously fired.

From this point forward, Beck formed bands where he called the shots. In 1967, he formed the first Jeff Beck Group. The band included future Faces and Rolling Stones guitarist Ronnie Wood (on bass), pianist extraordinaire Nicky Hopkins, drummer Mickey Waller and a shy, little-known singer named Rod Stewart.

The band produced the landmark albums *Truth* in 1968 and *Beck-Ola* (albeit with a different drummer) in 1969. The Jeff Beck Group merged hi-decibel blues with sonically radical jams that became musical touchstones for Led Zeppelin, the Faces and metal bands to follow. But the notoriously impetuous guitarist ended the collaboration just prior to a scheduled appearance at Woodstock.

GENE SIMMONS: No one played guitar like Jeff. Please get ahold of the first two Jeff Beck Group albums and behold greatness.

In 1971, he formed the second Jeff Beck Group with a new supporting cast with roots in Memphis soul, rhythm 'n' blues and jazz. The albums *Rough and Ready* (1971) and *The Jeff Beck Group* (1972) hinted at new directions for the mercurial guitarist.

The ever-restless guitar slinger then moved quickly and formed his long-desired power trio with ex–Vanilla Fudge members Carmine Appice (drums/vocals) and Tim Bogart (bass/vocals). Despite good intentions, their 1973 studio effort—*Beck, Bogert and Appice*—was a musically plodding endeavor that ended quickly.

Beck was again on the move. He told *Guitar Player* magazine, "There's nothing worse than a boring sermon you already know." Taking his own advice, he broke new musical ground by seeking musicians who could better keep pace with his stylistic turns. As an admirer of the supercharged fusion band Mahavishnu Orchestra, Beck went all instrumental with the 1975 album *Blow by Blow*, his most commercially successful album.

The 1976 follow-up, *Wired*, was a more stripped-down effort that featured ex-Mahavishnu keyboardist Jan Hammer. *Wired* features some of the greatest guitar chops on record, and Beck's reputation continued to grow.

With a reputation for reclusiveness, Beck recorded sporadically over the next fifteen years. His vintage car hobby took priority. In 1980, he returned to familiar ground with another all-instrumental fusion workout, *There and Back*. His song "The Pump" is famously featured in the movie *Risky Business*.

Over the years, Beck would radically change his playing technique by doing away with a guitar pick and replacing it with finger plucking. He further explored a range of sonic possibilities through a variety of techniques best left for guitar magazines to explain.

In 1985, he switched gears again by bringing back vocals to his techno-pop album *Flash* (the song "Escape" won a Grammy for Best Instrumental Performance). But the recording's high point was Curtis Mayfield's classic "People Get Ready" with Rod Stewart on vocals.

Four years later, he returned to an all-instrumental format with *Jeff Beck's Guitar Shop*. Beck again displayed a wide range of styles and industrial-like atmospherics.

From 1989 on, Jeff slowly ramped-up his visibility, recording projects and touring. Along with frequent benefit appearances, Beck contributed his talents to recording artists such as Stevie Wonder, Buddy Guy, Tina Turner, Mick Jagger and Ozzy Osbourne.

He continued to follow his muse wherever it took him, including guitar interpretations of classical music and opera. Always full of surprises, Beck showcased budding and veteran female vocalists, guitarists, bassists and drummers in his bands.

His final project—an album and tour with actor/musician Johnny Depp—preceded Beck's sudden death from bacterial meningitis on January 11, 2023.

Shortly after Jeff's passing, his wife, Sandra, and Eric Clapton organized two memorial concerts at London's Royal Albert Hall. Jeff once said, "I was going to write an autobiography once. I started writing it, and then I thought, 'No, let them dig around when I'm dead.'"

No digging needed. Just put needle on vinyl.

MUSICAL INFLUENCES WHO MATTER

Les Paul, Cliff Gallup, James Burton, Steve Cropper, Ravi Shankar, Roy Buchanan, Chet Atkins, Django Reinhardt, Lonnie Mack, John McLaughlin, Jan Hammer, Barney Kessel, Otis Rush, Buddy Guy, Freddie King, B.B. King, Michael Bloomfield, Peter Green.

PROBABLE CONCERT SETLIST: ARIE CROWN THEATER, MAY 8, 1975

"Constipated Duck," "She's a Woman," "Freeway Jam," "Definitely Maybe," "Superstition," "Cause We've Ended as Lovers," "Power," "Got the Feeling," "Diamond Dust," "You Know What I Mean."

ERIC CLAPTON

GUITAR, VOCALS, SONGWRITER, BANDLEADER, FILM SCORES

EDDIE VAN HALEN: Eric Clapton is basically the only guitar player who influenced me even though I don't sound like him. His solos were melodic and memorable and that's what guitar solos should be...part of the song. Those solos are permanently imprinted in my brain. That blues-based sound is still the core of modern rock guitar.

WHY HE MATTERS

At age sixteen, Eric Patrick Clapton was "released" from Surrey's Kingston Art College due to his preoccupation with the guitar and blues music. Four years later, fans were scribbling "Clapton is God" on the street and subway walls of London. It is this kind of adulation that EC has both embraced and run from his entire career.

ERIC CLAPTON: I didn't want that kind of notoriety as I knew it would bring some kind of trouble....Another part of me really liked the idea that what I had been fostering all these years was finally getting some kind of recognition.

From birth, Clapton was destined to find solace and purpose in the blues. His grandmother Rose Clapp told *Life* magazine in 1971, "He was always a lonely boy, and his music still gives me that feeling about him."

Eric Clapton.

Appreciating Clapton's career requires familiarity with his personal life. He grew up thinking that his grandparents were his parents and his birth mother was his sister. He went from a shy and insecure youth to an idolized musician whose all-consuming love for Patti Harrison led to a legendary rock album and battle with heroin. Then came recovery, alcoholism, sobriety and the tragic death of his four-year-old son, Conor. But Clapton always managed to turn his personal blues into inspiration.

Two musicians who had the strongest pull on his music and guitar playing were bluesmen Robert Johnson and Freddie King.

> **ERIC CLAPTON:** Robert Johnson was the most important blues musician who ever lived. His music remains the most powerful cry that I think you can find in the human voice. It seemed to echo something I had always felt.

In 1963, Clapton began his recording career with the Yardbirds. Following the release of the band's 1965 pop hit "For Your Love," Clapton went searching for a purer blues experience. He found it with John Mayall and the Bluesbreakers. It was here that Eric changed the way lead guitarists would play and sound. With a Gibson Les Paul and Marshall amp in overdrive, Clapton achieved a fat, electrifying guitar tone that embellished his six-string artistry.

> **ROLLING STONE MAGAZINE:** Although barely in his 20s, this is still his finest moment as a blues player. His performances on this set are frightening. On track after track, he tears off devastating solos. The high point is "Have You Heard," a six-minute slow blues on which every note he plays is shattering.

Ever restless, "Slowhand" needed a band of his own and one that could move the blues forward. In 1966, he joined forces with multi-instrumentalist Jack Bruce and drummer Ginger Baker—both well known for their instrumental virtuosity. In the studio, Cream was a tight, sophisticated unit that employed poetic imagery and orchestration to compositions like "White Room." They also covered blues classics. But on stage, Dr. Jekyll turned into Mr. Hyde. Cream improvised lengthy muscular jams that incorporated blues, jazz and near-metal rock. They defined the rock power trio and in their finest moments, brought awe and respectability to rock musicianship.

STEVEN VAN ZANDT: When all his creativity, passion, frustration and anger came together, it was frightening. His solo on "Crossroads" is impossible. I don't know how he kept time while he played. Anyone who plays lead guitar owes him a debt of gratitude. He wrote the fundamental code, the binary language that everyone uses to this day.

After two and a half years, Clapton grew tired of soloing, idolatry and keeping the peace between Baker and Bruce. In late 1968, Cream called it quits with a final goodbye concert at London's Royal Albert Hall.

Blind Faith came next—a well-intended effort that fell short. The collaboration of Clapton, Steve Winwood, Ginger Baker and Rick Grech quickly collapsed under the weight of supergroup expectations. But Blind Faith's only album reached no. 1 in the United States and United Kingdom and produced lasting songs that Clapton and Winwood cover to this day.

At this juncture, Clapton retreated into the background by guesting or touring with others, including John Lennon's Plastic Ono Band and George Harrison. He continued to view himself as an incomplete musician but gained confidence in his singing and songwriting abilities thanks to Delaney Bramlett's encouragement. The result was his first solo album, *Eric Clapton*, featuring the classics "Let It Rain" and "After Midnight."

Clapton's solos were aggressive but more concise. Now that he was playing a Fender Stratocaster, his riffs took on a more "raw and metallic" tone. It was also during this period that he fell in love with the wife of a Beatle. Clapton was about to experience the blues more intensely than ever.

With his band Derek and the Dominos, Clapton channeled unrequited love into a masterpiece. With Duane Allman in the studio, Eric was motivated to play his heart out. *Layla and Other Assorted Long Songs* remains one of the greatest rock albums of all time.

PRODUCER TOM DOWD: There had to be some sort of telepathy going on [between Eric and Duane] because I've never seen spontaneous inspiration happen at that rate and level.

Drowning in a sea of drugs and booze, the band fell apart during the making of a second album. It was here that Clapton plunged into heroin addiction and nearly three years of isolation. Pete Townshend managed to briefly lure him out. Clapton was devastated that his proudest recording initially received lukewarm reviews.

If Eric's career had ended here, he would have been a twice-inducted Rock & Roll Hall of Famer. But he had one more induction coming as a solo artist. In 1974, a "clean" and healthier-looking Clapton emerged with a no. 1 studio album, *461 Ocean Boulevard*. Unfortunately, Eric turned to drinking and recorded several soft albums over the next ten years. Nevertheless, his guitar chops emerged on albums like *Slowhand, August, Journeyman* and the live *24 Nights*.

During this period, Clapton became active in several charity and tribute events. In the 1990s, tragedy struck again. Following an outdoor concert with Robert Cray and Stevie Ray Vaughan, three of Clapton's crew along with Vaughan died when their helicopter crashed into a ski hill in Wisconsin.

Shortly thereafter, Clapton's four-year-old son, Conor, fell to his death from an open high-rise window. As he had done in the past, Clapton responded to tragedy with a worldwide hit, "Tears in Heaven."

In the mid-1990s, Clapton returned to his muse by making an album of blues covers. *From the Cradle* became a no. 1 multiplatinum seller with some of Clapton's most inspired guitar playing and singing in years.

Years later, Clapton paid tribute to his idol, Robert Johnson, with the album *Me and Mr. Johnson* (with companion DVD). With his voice well-toned from years of smoking, substance abuse and age, Clapton felt he could do proper justice to Johnson's music.

Around this time, Clapton launched the first of his many Crossroads Guitar Festivals that bring together top guitar talent on one stage. The festival raises money for his Antigua-based drug rehab facility.

From 2005 to 2010, EC tied up several loose ends and fulfilled the dreams of many fans. In 2005, Cream reunited for several concerts in London and New York.

METALLICA'S KIRK HAMMETT: It was like 1968 again. They were vibrating, establishing eye contact and pushing the limits. Music is about chemistry, and it was so evident with them. I doubt they played that way with anyone else since last playing together.

In 2008, Clapton and Steve Winwood took care of unfinished business by touring and performing the music of Blind Faith, Traffic, Derek and the Dominos and others. Two years later and to the delight of guitar worshippers, Clapton and Jeff Beck joined forces for several shows.

A few years later, EC honored the passing of legendary blues guitarist Hubert Sumlin by assembling special guests for a memorial concert at New York's famed Apollo Theater

Over his career, few rock 'n' roll musicians have commanded so much respect from their peers. Time will tell if the legend has paid his debt to the mythical devil at Robert Johnson's crossroads.

MUSICAL INFLUENCES WHO MATTER

Buddy Holly, Chuck Berry, Little Richard, Jerry Lee Lewis, Little Walter, Freddie King, B.B. King, Albert King, Buddy Guy, Otis Rush, Hubert Sumlin, Jimi Hendrix, Robert Johnson, John Lee Hooker, Bukka White, Howlin' Wolf, Muddy Waters, Willie Dixon, Elmore James, Wes Montgomery, Blind Willie McTell, Thelonius Monk, Leroy Carr, Blind Lemon Jefferson, Big Bill Broonzy, Ray Charles, Louis Armstrong, Mississippi John Hurt.

PROBABLE CONCERT SETLIST:
INTERNATIONAL AMPHITHEATER, JULY 2, 1974

"Smile," "Let It Grow," "Can't Find My Way Home," "Blues Power," "Have You Ever Loved a Woman," "Tell the Truth," "Layla," "Willie and the Hand Jive," "Get Ready," "Let It Rain," "Key to the Highway," "Presence of the Lord," "Cross Road Blues."

B.B. KING

GUITAR, SINGER, SONGWRITER, BANDLEADER

B.B. KING: The blues are simple music, and I'm a simple man. But the blues aren't a science; the blues can't be broken down like mathematics. The blues are a mystery and mysteries are never as simple as they look.

WHY HE MATTERS

To blues aficionados, the surname King represents the trifecta of blues guitar. While Albert and Freddie King were pivotal figures whose influence on British and American guitar players is legendary, B.B. King is universally recognized as the most accomplished practitioner and ambassador of post–World War II blues. King brought the genre from the margins to the mainstream.

BILLY GIBBONS: He goes back far enough to remember the sound of the field hollers and cornerstone blues figures like Charley Patton and Robert Johnson.

Over a career spanning seven decades, B.B. King amassed an exhaustive list of honors and awards. He played the blues in eighty-eight countries, and his impassioned, powerful falsetto and impressive vocal range made a believer out of the most jaded listener. His economical single-note guitar bursts, string bends and left-hand vibrato have become the building blocks of modern rock and blues guitar.

In 1998, Buddy Guy told *Mojo* magazine, "Before him, everyone played guitar like it was an acoustic. B.B. is the father of the squeezing of the string of the electric guitar. You could say he invented lead guitar. I often say every electric guitar they make should have a 'B' on it."

King was born to a family of poor sharecroppers during the Great Depression. His parents separated when he was four, and his mother died five years later. In 1943, he took off for Indianola, Mississippi, where he worked as a tractor driver and performed in a gospel quartet. Over the next few years, he bounced around Indianola and Memphis, Tennessee, to pursue a music career.

His first break came at radio station KWEM in West Memphis, where King performed on Sonny Boy Williamson's program. Meanwhile, a rival radio station across town was seeking to attract a Black audience. King was hired as a disc jockey and took on the moniker "Beale Street Blues Boy," later shortened to "B.B." With King aboard, WDIA became the first station in the South to be operated by an all-Black staff.

In 1949, WDIA helped King make his first professional recording. A few years after, he landed a multiyear recording contract with the help of talent scout Ike Turner. His first rhythm 'n' blues chart topper was a version of Lowell Fulson's "Three O' Clock Blues." Throughout his career, King demonstrated a knack for putting his individual stamp on songs written by others.

Eventually, King left his radio show and local gig for a hectic bus touring schedule—a practice that continued well into his eighties and helped build his reputation. By the mid-1950s, King was scoring hit after hit on the rhythm 'n' blues chart and had become one of the top attractions on the "Chitlin' Circuit."

While other Black artists such as Fats Domino and Chuck Berry were crossing over, King could not yet relate to rock 'n' roll. That would change. Until then, King continued to grind it out on the road. His next big move arrived in 1961, when he signed with ABC Records—a company that had previously landed Ray Charles. Under ABC's guidance, King's sound grew in terms of supporting instrumentation. In 1965, he scored his first Billboard Hot 100 entry with "How Blue Can You Get." The song is famous for its biting lyrics and surefire audience reaction:

> *I gave you a brand-new Ford, but you said I want a Cadillac…I bought you a ten-dollar dinner and you said thanks for the snack…I let you live in my penthouse but you said it was just a shack…I gave you seven children and now you wanna give 'em back!*

B.B. King.

In November 1964, B.B. recorded a groundbreaking live album in Chicago titled *Live at the Regal*. British historian Colin Escott described the concert as "a peek into the church revival blues experience where performer and audience feed off each other's energy."

King's audience was changing. Prominent rock bands were now introducing their audiences to American blues. King was now playing college campuses, rock ballrooms and music festivals. And while he was scoring with a new audience, he continued to be popular with his old fan base, but not so with young Black listeners.

> **B.B. KING:** Well, I was watching TV one night and the lead singer of the Beatles—John Lennon—said he wished he could play like B.B. King. I almost fell out of my chair. The greatest group on earth and that guy is saying that [about] me?

It was at this point that King realized his style was having far greater influence than he imagined. In 1968, King had crossover success with the single "Paying the Cost to Be the Boss" and later 1970's "The Thrill Is Gone." The latter won King the first of fifteen Grammy Awards and marked a turning point in his career. The albums *Live and Well* and *Completely Well* had also crossed over. He appeared on *The Ed Sullivan Show* and *Johnny Carson's Tonight Show*. He opened for the Rolling Stones and would later appear in Las Vegas. He found his music reaching more people than it had in all years prior.

King's long-lasting success owes to his growth as a musician and quest to be his best. With his crack horn section and obediently tight supporting bands, King fused traditional blues, gospel, jazz, swing and pop. His early, raw sound became more sophisticated and polished with horns and strings.

King went on to cut several albums with admirers and peers, including the Grammy-winning *Riding with the King* with Eric Clapton. Although a long way from his simple beginnings, King was always protective of the music that made him what he was.

> **B.B. KING:** Things people used to say about the blues singers that I thought of as greats used to hurt me. They spoke of them as illiterate and dirty. The blues had made me a better living than any I had, so this was when I really put my fight on.

King passed away on May 14, 2015. When the news broke, the world of social media exploded with words of praise, respect and sadness and from the unlikeliest of individuals. Meghan McCain—the daughter of the late senator John McCain—wrote on Twitter, "The first time I got my heart broken, it was B.B. King's music that expressed emotions I couldn't."

B.B. once remarked, "I'm trying to get people to see that we are our brother's keeper. Red, white, black, brown, yellow, rich or poor, we all have the blues."

Even Meghan McCain.

MUSICAL INFLUENCES WHO MATTER

T-Bone Walker, Charlie Christian, Louis Jordan, Count Basie, Django Reinhardt, Blind Lemon Jefferson, Lonnie Johnson, Bukka White, Lester Young, Robert Nighthawk, Johnny Hodges, Leon McAuliffe, Frank Sinatra, Nat "King" Cole, Frankie Lane, Vaughn Monroe.

PROBABLE CONCERT SETLIST: KINETIC PLAYGROUND, MARCH 30, 1973

"The Thrill Is Gone," "Every Day I Have the Blues," "All Over Now," "I Got Some Outside Help (I Don't Really Need)," "King's Shuffle," "Guess Who," "Nobody Loves Me But My Mother," "Sweet Little Angel," "Ain't Nobody Home."

JOHNNY WINTER

GUITAR, VOCALS, SONGWRITER, BANDLEADER

PROGRESSIVE BLUES EXPERIMENT LINER NOTES: Before the recording session, there was Johnny and his guitar. During the session, Johnny became the guitar.

WHY HE MATTERS

Johnny Winter always stood out in a crowd. He had albinism; long, whitish hair; a cross-eyed gaze; and an illustrated body. But with a guitar slung around his neck, the man stood out even more. No white musician was more passionate for so long in keeping the blues alive and well.

The songs on *Progressive Blues Experiment* are the embodiment of every country and urban bluesman that came before him. His unmistakable voice—alternating between throaty pronouncements and convincingly sung lyrics—was a powerful tool in his blues bag.

After kicking around bands with his brother Edgar (keyboards and sax), Johnny's life shifted dramatically in 1968. Guitarist Michael Bloomfield enthusiastically introduced Winter to the audience at a 1968 Fillmore East concert with "This is the baddest motherfucker." A *Rolling Stone* magazine article anointed him the next great Texas axman. Shortly thereafter, wannabe managers and record labels scrambled to sign him.

Johnny Winter.

In 1969, he reached a $600,000 deal with Columbia (CBS) Records for what then was a record sum of money—remarkable for a blues-oriented artist. His first album for Columbia was simply called *Johnny Winter*. The album featured brother Edgar and two blues legends: Walter "Shakey" Horton and Willie Dixon. Rounding out the band was drummer Uncle John Turner and future Stevie Ray Vaughan bassist Tommy Shannon.

His next Columbia album, *Second Winter*, pushed more of his rock 'n' roll influences to the forefront. His breakneck version of Dylan's "Highway 61 Revisited" is a primer on slide guitar, and his echo-drenched wah-wah on "The Good Love" sounds like a pack of yelping hellhounds on his trail.

Johnny's complete transition to rock 'n' roll came next with the group Johnny Winter And. The "And" included members of the McCoys, a pop group who scored the hit "Hang on Sloopy." Despite their pop origins, guitarist and producer Rick Derringer and his bandmates were worthy rockers. Unfortunately for Johnny, the "And" years were accompanied by heroin addiction and depression. After several lost years, he returned by recording the album *Still Alive and Well.*

JOHNNY WINTER SINGS: I'm still alive and well, I'm still alive and well, every now and then I know it's kind of hard to tell but I'm still alive and well....I'm here to stay.

With a new lease on life, he collaborated with his idol Muddy Waters on four highly regarded blues albums that reintroduced and revitalized Water's career. The Grammy-winning album *Hard Again* features the timeless blues anthem "Mannish Boy." His feel for the original Waters sound made these albums special and led Muddy to call Johnny his adopted son.

Winter's rededication to the blues came in 1984 when he signed with Chicago's Alligator Records. Two of his three releases were Grammy nominated, and *Guitar Slinger* was widely acclaimed. It also spawned his first music video, which received six months of rotation on the fledgling MTV network.

Winter continued to record but was hampered by years of mismanagement and poor health. In 2005, musician Paul Nelson took official control of Johnny's career out of respect for the fading bluesman. As a result, Winter became healthier and reestablished his career with several new releases and tours. Most notable was the release of *Live Bootleg Series (1–8)*, an officially sanctioned and remastered series of vintage Winter performances.

Sadly, the Texan from Beaumont passed away in his hotel in Switzerland during a 2014 world tour. The posthumously released album *Step Back* won a Grammy in 2015. It features Eric Clapton, Joe Walsh, Dr. John, mandolinist David Grisman, Mark Knopfler and others.

John Dawson Winter III was never comfortable with the guitar god label. In his biography *Raisin' Cain*, he was asked how he'd like to be remembered. He responded, "As a good blues player."

Winter was better than just good. He was the first non–African American artist inducted into the Blues Foundation Hall of Fame and was selected as best blues guitarist three times by *Guitar Player* magazine.

MUSICAL INFLUENCES WHO MATTER

Son House, Robert Johnson, Sonny Terry, Muddy Waters, Willie Dixon, Little Walter, B.B. King, T-Bone Walker, Elmore James, Lightning Hopkins, Jimmy Reed, John Lee Hooker, Clarence "Gatemouth" Brown, Chuck Berry, Little Richard.

PROBABLE CONCERT SETLIST: AUDITORIUM THEATRE, FEBRUARY 27, 1975

"Rock and Roll People," "Roll with Me," "Stranger," "Bony Moronie," "Sweet Papa John," "Keep Me Satisfied," "Highway 61 Revisited," "Johnny B. Goode," "Jumpin' Jack Flash," "Roll Over Beethoven," "It's All Over Now."

EDGAR WINTER

MULTI-INSTRUMENTALIST, SINGER, BANDLEADER, COMPOSER, ARRANGER

EDGAR WINTER: Looking different had its advantages in the world of rock 'n' roll.

WHY HE MATTERS

As children, Edgar and Johnny were inseparable, and their foray into music was linked together. But Johnny was destined to be the family's guitar man and unofficial torch carrier for the blues. Edgar was more withdrawn and introspective and would initially be content to learn as many other instruments as possible to support his brother's bands.

By the time Edgar Winter left his hometown in the late 1960s, he was technically proficient in many forms of music. And while Johnny's muse was the blues, Edgar gravitated toward jazz and the alto sax.

EDGER WINTER: A lot of bands at the time like Otis Redding, Ray Charles and even B.B. King had horns. When I picked up the sax, Johnny said, "I don't want no saxophone in my band." I was like "OK, I'll get my own band then."

In 1968, Johnny was scooped up by New York music entrepreneur Steve Paul and signed to Columbia Records. Edgar assisted in rehearsing and writing charts for Johnny's first album but was encouraged to record music of his own. As a result, Edgar signed with Epic Records and received the blessing of CBS president Clive Davis to make records following his own instincts. The result was Edgar's experimental debut album *Entrance*, on which Edgar played most of the instruments.

The brothers were now traveling separate musical paths. In 1971, Edgar formed the band White Trash with a sound rooted in the roadhouse music of the Southwest. It was one of the most underappreciated white horn bands ever assembled. Their debut album received critical praise and a year later was followed by a double live album of seminal progressive rock called *Roadwork*. Despite achieving gold sales certification, Edgar disbanded the group.

He then assembled a quintessential American rock 'n' roll band named the Edgar Winter Group. Among the members were singer-songwriter Dan Hartman, guitarist Ronnie Montrose and guitarist Rick Derringer, who later replaced Montrose.

The Edgar Winter Group made two successful albums: *They Only Come Out at Night* (1972) and *Shock Treatment* (1974). More than anything, the band is remembered for the monster instrumental hit "Frankenstein" and the ubiquitous party tune "Free Ride." The synthesizer-heavy "Frankenstein" became a no. 1 hit. Over the years, "Free Ride" has become a familiar figure in movies, television shows and ad campaigns.

> **EDGAR WINTER:** I always loved those synthesized sounds in old Sci-Fi movies like *Forbidden Planet*. One day, I was browsing a music store and came across an ARP 2600 synthesizer. I thought, "Wow, looks like you could attach a strap to that and play it like a guitar," which I proceeded to do.

The making of "Frankenstein" is a story unto itself. Years earlier, Edgar devised the song's main riff as part of a live jam performed with his brother Johnny. With the tape machines rolling, the Edgar Winter Group performed endless live takes. Guitarist-producer Rick Derringer suggested they edit those jams into something tangible.

> **EDGAR WINTER:** It turned into one big editing party and an excuse to get blasted. And back then, the only way to edit recordings was to physically cut tape and splice pieces together....There was tape laying all over the control room.

Edgar Winter.

The song's title came from a remark made by drummer Chuck Ruff, who mumbled the immortal words, "Wow man, it's like Frankenstein."

Although Edgar never replicated his 1970s popularity, he has never stopped making music or venturing into other artistic areas. Years later, Edgar and Johnny would join forces on tour.

When his brother died in 2014, Edgar aired his feelings publicly: "Johnny has always been and will forever remain my greatest musical hero. But more than all that, he's my brother in family, in music and in life and beyond." In 2022, Edgar Winter released a star-studded seventeen-song tribute album titled *Brother Johnny*.

MUSICAL INFLUENCES WHO MATTER

Ray Charles, B.B. King, Bobby Blue Bland, Wilson Pickett, Sam Cooke, Jackie Wilson, Lou Rawls, Charlie Parker, Otis Redding, John Coltrane, Miles Davis, Glenn Miller, Gene Krupa, Benny Goodman, Artie Shaw, Cannonball Adderley, Hank Crawford, Little Richard, Chuck Berry, Doctor John, Professor Longhair, Billy Preston, the Beatles.

PROBABLE CONCERT SETLIST:
INTERNATIONAL AMPHITHEATER, JULY 9, 1974

"Keep Playin' That Rock 'n' Roll," "River's Risin'," "Hangin' Around," "Do Like Me," "Uncomplicated," "Easy Street," "Free Ride," "Rock 'n' Roll Hoochie Koo," "Teenage Love Affair," "Frankenstein," "Undercover Man," "Nu'Orlins/Long Tall Sally."

RICK DERRINGER

GUITAR, SINGER, SONGWRITER, PRODUCER

WHY HE MATTERS

Richard Zehringer was born August 5, 1947, in Fort Recovery, Ohio. The inspiration for his stage name Derringer came from the pistol logo used by his first record label, Bang Records.

Sandwiched between his 1960s pop stardom and later forays into smooth jazz and Christian music, Rick Derringer helped craft the vintage hard rock sound of the 1970s. His guitar, songwriting, voice and studio production skills served not only the bands he led but also a wide range of big-name rockers and some inconceivable partnerships like the World Wrestling Federation.

In the mid-1950s, Elvis Presley, Little Richard and Jerry Lee Lewis gave the nine-year-old Zehringer ideas. He got a guitar, passed around a hat and made forty-three bucks. This marked the unofficial beginning of his professional career.

Four years later, Rick and his younger brother Randy (who played drums) convinced a neighbor to learn bass guitar. The first song they taught him was the Ventures' "The McCoy." That song title would become the band's name.

In 1965, the McCoys recorded their breakthrough song "Hang on Sloopy." It rocketed to no. 1 in the United States, but its popularity reached well beyond America's shores. In fact, it penetrated the Soviet Union's Iron Curtain.

Rick Derringer.

Over the next four years, the McCoys toured with a revised lineup and recorded several albums. They had one more high-charting single, but the band was categorized as pop and bubblegum at a time when the music was getting heavier.

Around 1969, the McCoys' predicament changed when Johnny and Edgar Winter saw them perform in concert. Derringer told Janne Stark of *Fuzz* magazine, "We were not the lightweight band portrayed by our records. We were a pretty heavy weight band which is why Johnny and Edgar liked us."

Johnny Winter's manager Steve Paul saw an opportunity to merge Johnny's underground blues with the McCoys populist rock 'n' roll.

> **RICK DERRINGER:** We wanted a way to gain credibility. Johnny came on the scene with some real respect, so we looked at this as an opportunity to get what we were looking for—some respect for ourselves!

And so, the Johnny Winter And band was born in 1970. The band released one studio album featuring the original version of Rick Derringer's later hit "Rock and Roll Hoochie Koo." Next came a blistering live album (*Live*) showcasing Rick and Johnny's tour-de-force rhythm and lead guitar exchanges. Although Derringer would contribute to additional Johnny Winter albums, Johnny temporarily retired as his drug dependency worsened. Derringer's influence as a player, songwriter and producer carried over to Edgar Winter and his bands White Trash and the Edger Winter Group.

In 1973, Derringer launched his solo career with the LP *All American Boy*. It was here that Derringer rolled out his version of the monster rocker "Rock and Roll Hoochie Koo." Unfortunately, this underappreciated album fell through the cracks, and some argue the glam cover artwork didn't help.

Between 1976 and 1978, Derringer released several hard-driving rock albums with his band Derringer. However, album sales never matched the band's concert popularity. The 1977 album *Live* showcased the group at its best with Rick's singing and guitar work at its peak.

Derringer also found time for plenty of session work with everyone from Steely Dan and Meatloaf to Cyndi Lauper and Bette Midler. Perhaps most surprising was his guitar and production work for Grammy-winning comic "Weird Al" Yankovic, best known for his Michael Jackson video parodies.

The native Ohioan maintained a low profile between the years 1983 and 1993. He returned to the studio with a series of four blues albums where he cut loose with vintage blues-rock fury. He also resumed his music-making relationship with Edgar Winter before joining up with ex–Vanilla Fudge stars Tim Bogert and Carmine Appice to form the band DBA.

In 2002, Derringer found a new avenue for his music. He released *Free Ride*, a smooth jazz instrumental album that showcased another side of his musicianship. He then turned to family and Christian music without abandoning rock 'n' roll.

He explained to Tom Guerra of *Vintage Guitar* magazine; "A few years back, I went through a terrible time, and I started praying for answers and got them. Part of that was finding [wife] Brenda. I know some people will be surprised to hear it, but I've found that my music, whether its blues or rock or whatever you call it, can be channeled into a positive direction that actually helps people. I never knew music could have such power."

MUSICAL INFLUENCES WHO MATTER

Elvis Presley, Little Richard, Jerry Lee Lewis, Django Reinhardt, Les Paul, Chet Atkins, Wes Montgomery, Jimi Hendrix.

PROBABLE CONCERT SETLIST:
INTERNATIONAL AMPHITHEATER, JULY 9, 1974
(PERFORMED WITH THE EDGAR WINTER GROUP)

"Keep Playin' That Rock 'n' Roll," "River's Risin'," "Hangin' Around," "Do Like Me," "Uncomplicated," "Easy Street," "Free Ride," "Rock and Roll Hoochie Koo," "Teenage Love Affair," "Frankenstein," "Undercover Man," "Nu'Orlins/Long Tall Sally."

Kim Simmonds.

SAVOY BROWN

FORMED 1966

BAND MEMBERS WHO MATTER

Kim Simmonds (guitar, vocals, piano, harmonica), Chris Youlden (vocals, piano), Dave Peverett (guitar, vocals), Roger Earl (drums), Bob Hall (piano), Tony Stevens (bass), Bob Brunning (bass), Garnett Grim (drums), Pat DeSalvo (bass, vocals).

> KIM SIMMONDS: We were one of the first bands to capture that authentic feel. A lot of the blues artists we jammed with at the time were quite surprised at our grasp of the blues, so when we came over, the older established guys seemed to embrace us as did the fans.

WHY THEY MATTER

During the 1960s, the London underground scene was teeming with blues and rock talent. One of those cornerstone acts—and one of the most underappreciated—was Savoy Brown. Founded in 1966 by a nineteen-year-old Welsh blues guitarist named Kim Simmonds, Savoy Brown exported blues music back to the United States that invigorated the art form and called attention to forgotten blues artists.

For Simmonds and like-minded musicians, playing the blues was a labor of love. It was certainly not a fast track to riches. Although the band fell short of superstar status, they achieved what few blues bands could—they penetrated the pop charts by breaking through Billboard's "Top 100" several times. The band's first album, *Shakedown*, was a U.K.-only release and the only album by original members. A year later, the LP *Getting to the Point* expanded on the band's basic formula and marked the beginning of countless personnel changes.

Sharing the spotlight with Simmonds was a new standout vocalist who also shared writing duties. His name was Chris Youlden, a young man with a "living-hard" look and an alchemistic singing voice. The addition of pianist Bob Hall bolstered the band's blues credentials with his Albert Ammons and Otis Spann playing style.

In 1969, the band entered what many consider their classic period. Over the next three years, Savoy Brown released five LPs, toured America six times and shared bills with legendary bands at some of the era's most famous venues. Although several lineups were responsible for this period's studio and live releases, the one dearest to fans included founder and mainstay Kim Simmonds, Chris Youlden, "Lonesome" Dave Peverett, Roger Earl, Tony Stevens and Bob Hall.

This ensemble released three memorable albums and several singles over a two-year period. *Blue Matter*, *A Step Further* and *Raw Sienna* showcased some of Savoy Brown's best songwriting, singing and musicianship. Several songs featured string and brass arrangements that embellished the band's sound. The result was a creative brew of hard-driving rock, boogie, juke joint blues, ballads and jazzy excursions. Few bands played or sounded like Savoy Brown.

In 1971, Chris Youlden split for a solo career, and the remaining band members recorded the album *Looking In*. But Peverett, Earl and Stevens moved on to form the band Foghat. Despite the good-natured jokes about the band's history of personnel changes, Simmonds viewed these as positive and necessary to keep the music fresh.

Next came the 1971 release *Street Corner Talking*. It was one of the band's most accessible with catchy tunes like "Street Corner Talking," "Tell Mama," "I Can't Get Next to You" and "Wang Dang Doodle." The final LP from the band's classic period was *Hellbound Train*.

From 1973 to 2000, Simmonds continued to tap myriad musicians to perform and record under the Savoy Brown banner. In the new millennium, Simmonds ventured into the realm of acoustic music and released several solo albums, including his 2008 confessional CD, *Out of the Blue*.

In 2010, Simmonds again proved that finding the right combination of players and chemistry was the key to Savoy Brown's vitality. The Welshman put together his most potent lineup since the band's classic years. The 2011 release *Voodoo Moon* was enthusiastically received by fans and featured singer/saxophonist Joe Whiting, bassist Pat DeSalvo, drummer Garnett Grim and studio keyboardist Andy Rudy. DeSalvo and Grim would remain with Simmonds for the next twelve years.

The saga of Savoy Brown ended when Kim Simmonds passed away on December 13, 2022. He wanted to be remembered as one of the best guitar players in the world. When Jim Summaria—co-host of *That Classic Rock Show*—asked Kim if he knew Jimi Hendrix, he responded, "Know Jimi Hendrix? I jammed with Jimi Hendrix!" Enough said.

MUSICAL INFLUENCES WHO MATTER

Bill Haley, Howlin' Wolf, Hubert Sumlin, Earl Hooker, Freddy King, Matt "Guitar" Murphy, Otis Rush, Muddy Waters, Lightning Hopkins, Chuck Berry, Eric Clapton, Peter Green (original Fleetwood Mac), the Rolling Stones, Yardbirds, Paul Butterfield Blues Band.

PROBABLE CONCERT SETLIST:
AUDITORIUM THEATRE, OCTOBER 19, 1975

"Wang Dang Doodle," "Tell Mama," "Hellbound Train," "Hero to Zero," "Savoy Brown Boogie," "I Can't Get Next to You," "Louisiana Blues," "All I Can Do Is Try."

FOGHAT

FORMED 1971

BAND MEMBERS WHO MATTER

Dave Peverett (lead vocals, guitar), Rod Price (vocals, guitar, slide guitar), Tony Stevens (bass), Roger Earl (drums).

> ROGER EARL: In another thirty-five years, we'll have been around seventy years. It would be cool if somebody said, "You should have seen Foghat. What a rock 'n' roll band!" Then maybe they'll put on *Live* or *Live 2* or *Fool for the City* and say, "Check this out, son!"

WHY THEY MATTER

Foghat's brand of blues, rock and boogie made them icons of 1970s rock. Their songs found their way from record vinyl and arenas to television shows, movies, video games and product advertising. Eight of their albums went gold while two others went platinum and double platinum. Even today, their hits remain a staple of FM and satellite rock radio.

The origins of Foghat go back to 1969 during a Savoy Brown recording session. While on break, members Dave Peverett, Tony Stevens and Roger Earl jammed rockabilly tunes for fun. About a year later, the three left Savoy Brown to pursue their own musical vision. They recruited Rod Price, a menacing-sounding slide guitarist with a solid blues résumé. Foghat was born.

"Lonesome" Dave Peverett.

At a time when the British blues boom was ending and record companies were focusing on singer/songwriters, Foghat pushed ahead with music that eventually connected with fans who scorned disco and new wave.

Their initial year was challenging, but Bob Dylan's manager, Albert Grossman, signed the quartet to his Bearsville Records label and, according to Roger Earl, "saved our lives."

Foghat's 1972 self-titled debut album yielded a steroid-infused version of Willie Dixon's "I Just Want to Make Love to You." It featured the band's trademark boogie beat along with call and response guitars that sounded like alley cats in heat. And for added measure, "Lonesome" Dave Peverett's overdriven vocal made Dixon's original version sound prudish.

Rod Price.

The band hit the road and built a sizeable following with their high-intensity performances. Over the next two years, the band released three credible albums. In 1975, Foghat experienced its first defection when bassist Tony Stevens left to pursue other interests. Nonetheless, the band gained strength by adding Nick Jameson, a gifted musician and producer.

The album *Fool for the City* was the quartet's commercial breakthrough and gave birth to the rock classics "Fool for the City" and "Slow Ride." The album *Nightshift* followed and spawned two singles, including the Top 40 "Drivin' Wheel."

By 1977, a live Foghat album made perfect sense. The result was *Live*—the band's double platinum–selling album. The LP included inspired live performances of three studio classics. The live version of "I Just Want to Make Love to You" was released as a single and became their third best-selling tune.

Foghat continued to release albums and sell out venues into the late 1980s, but their audience and commercial fortunes tailed off with changing musical trends. Dave Peverett—the band's frontman—felt Foghat's sound needed updating, but not all were on board. Rod Price departed. A few years later, Peverett left for family life in England. Had Foghat run its course?

In 1993, the soundtrack of the cult movie classic *Dazed and Confused* included the Foghat songs "Slow Ride" and "I Just Want to Make Love to You." Interest in Foghat was renewed. With the encouragement of hip-hop producer Rick Rubin, the original members reunited and recorded the 1994 LP *Return of the Boogie Men* and resumed touring.

In February 2000, the beloved Dave Peverett succumbed to complications from kidney cancer. Despite the passing of other members, drummer Roger Earl has kept Foghat's music alive with musicians who share the same passion and energy as those who started it all. In 2023—their fifty-second year—Foghat released a new album titled *Sonic Mojo*. Boogie like it's 1977!

MUSICAL INFLUENCES WHO MATTER

Bill Haley and the Comets, Jerry Lee Lewis, Carl Perkins, Elvis Presley, Fats Domino, Bo Diddley, Gene Vincent, Buddy Guy, Chuck Berry, Muddy Waters, Sonny Boy Williamson, John Lee Hooker, Big Bill Broonzy, Elmore James, Lightnin' Hopkins, Howlin' Wolf, Willie Dixon, Honey Boy Edwards.

PROBABLE CONCERT SETLIST:
AUDITORIUM THEATRE, AUGUST 19, 1974

"Road Fever," "Home in My Hand," "Golden Arrow," "Honey Hush," "Wild Cherry," "Leavin' Again," "I Just Want to Make Love to You," "Maybellene."

CLIMAX BLUES BAND

FORMED 1968

BAND MEMBERS WHO MATTER

Colin Cooper (vocals, sax, harmonica, rhythm guitar), Peter Haycock (guitar, vocals), Derek Holt (guitar, vocals, bass, keyboards), Arthur Wood (keyboards), Richard Jones (bass), George Newsome (drums), John Cuffley (drums).

> PETER HAYCOCK: It was quite acceptable to mix styles of the likes of Wilbert Harrison and Otis Rush with jazz, Cuban and even classical influences. It was a wonderful experience and it's sad that nobody makes records like that anymore.

WHY THEY MATTER

The original Chicago Climax Blues Band brought together an eclectic array of British musicians inspired by American Black music. The band's original name pointed to their greatest inspiration, yet it was their own material that lifted them to stardom years later.

In the early to mid-1960s, multi-instrumentalist Colin Cooper was honing his music skills in locally popular beat, jazz and rhythm 'n' blues outfits. He crossed paths with wunderkind guitarist Pete Haycock, who was inspired by the Shadows. Remember the 1960s hit instrumental "Apache"?

Left: Pete Haycock. *Right:* Derek Holt.

In 1967, Colin and Haycock formed a soul band but pinned their future on the last surge of British blues popularity. As a result, the Chicago Climax Blues Band (CCBB) was born. Their first album—released only in the United Kingdom—paid homage to American blues idols driven by Haycock's guitar skills.

Experimenting beyond traditional blues, they made *Plays On*, their first U.S. release. It barely cracked the Billboard 200. Over the next few years, CCBB released three solid LPs featuring an array of musical styles. Sales were steady but unremarkable. During this period, the band dropped Chicago from their name, and personnel changes followed.

In 1973, CBB focused on the lucrative U.S. market. The core group of Colin Cooper, Peter Haycock, Derek Holt and John Cuffley toured the country with supporting acts like Canned Heat and the Steve Miller Band.

Their breakthrough came with the release of *FM Live*, a double live LP that captured a live performance broadcast over New York City's WNEW-FM radio. The recording highlighted the band's jazz and blues chops and lingered on the Billboard 200 for thirty weeks.

CBB were now headliners. The core personnel on *FM Live* played together for eight years and represented the second-most enduring lineup in the band's history. The longest took place between 1993 and 2008.

Riding the coattails of *FM Live*, CBB released two solid studio albums: *Sense of Direction* in 1974 and *Stamp Album* in 1975. The albums featured a mixture of adult-oriented rock, funk, jazz, reggae and fine vocal harmonies between Cooper, Haycock and Holt. But seven years in, the band was still without a game-changing single.

In 1976, that all changed with the no. 3 hit "Couldn't Get it Right" written and sung by Colin Cooper. The catchy song chronicled life on the road. Riding on the song's commercial success, the album *Gold Plated* became the band's highest-charting LP.

Three more albums followed, and the veteran outfit left its blues roots behind for more mainstream pop-rock. But CBB remained popular in the United States, and in 1980, they again struck fortune with the single "I Love You" from the album *Flying the Flag*. Written and sung by bassist Derek Holt, the song has become a timeless staple of radio and wedding song requests.

More personnel changes followed. In 1981, the *Lucky for Some* album marked the last time Cooper, Haycock, Holt and Cuffley played as a unit. Album releases were sporadic over the next twelve years.

With Cooper as the only remaining original member, CBB released a live 1995 recording titled *Blues from the Attic*. Cooper's last CBB album—*Big Blues (The Songs of Willie Dixon)*—came in 2004 and brought CBB back full circle to the blues. Cooper died in 2008 and Peter Haycock in 2013.

Following his long tenure in CBB, Derek Holt's music making continued with *Night of the Guitars* featuring an all-star cast of name-familiar musicians. In addition to solo work and other collaborations, Holt briefly resurrected his version of the Climax Blues Band. But despite the band's pedigree, Holt said it was a hard sell for today's agents looking for fast and easy results.

MUSICAL INFLUENCES WHO MATTER

Hank Marvin, John Mayall's Bluesbreakers, Otis Rush, B.B. King, Albert King, Freddie King, Peter Green, Willie Dixon, Big Bill Broonzy, Muddy

Waters, Junior Wells, King Curtis, Junior Walker, David Sanborn, Sam Cooke, Mitch Mitchell, Buddy Rich, Tony Williams, Billy Preston, Jimmy Smith, Leonard Cohen, Herbie Hancock, Django Rheinhart, Stéphane Grappelli, Jeff Beck, Paul Kossoff, Rory Gallagher.

PROBABLE CONCERT SETLIST: AUDITORIUM THEATRE, OCTOBER 16, 1973

"All the Time in the World," "The Seventh Son," "Flight," "So Many Roads, So Many Trains," "Country Hat," "Shake Your Love," "Going to New York," "Let's Work Together," "One More Time/Stormy Monday."

RORY GALLAGHER

GUITARIST, MULTI-INSTRUMENTALIST, SINGER, SONGWRITER, BANDLEADER

BRIAN MAY: I owe Rory Gallagher my sound....I'd be the first to acknowledge a huge debt to the man.

WHY HE MATTERS

Death was the only thing that could come between Rory Gallagher and his guitar. But before it did, Rory achieved the dream of every musician: to make music on one's own terms, earn the respect of peers and bring joy to fans around the globe. In 1969, *Rolling Stone* magazine asked Jimi Hendrix what it felt like to be the world's greatest guitarist. Hendrix reportedly said, "I don't know, go ask Rory Gallagher."

Liam Rory Gallagher was born March 2, 1948, in Ballyshannon, Ireland. He was called a "workingman's musician" and "the people's guitarist." He was a gentle, no-nonsense soul who dressed like a laborer, shunned superficial stardom and avoided studio trickery. On stage, he swaggered and sweated until he could give no more.

Although never a household name, Gallagher developed a worldwide grassroots following through touring rather than hit singles. He performed three hundred or more gigs annually through much of his career, including twenty-five tours of the United States.

Rory was a master of both electric and acoustic six strings and sang like he carried the world's problems on his shoulders. His slide guitar skills

Rory Gallagher.

further enhanced his authentic blues credentials, although he wrote songs and played in a variety of genres.

As a preteen, Rory grew up without the benefit of a record player. His exposure to artists like Lonnie Donegan (the king of skiffle music), early rock 'n' rollers and blues masters came by way of television and radio.

At that time, Ireland was devoid of an "underground" music scene, making it difficult for like-minded musicians to collaborate. But Ireland had plenty of show bands that played dance and traditional music at ballrooms, pubs and army bases. At fifteen, Gallagher joined a show band as the token "young gun." He outgrew his sideman role but gained invaluable gigging experience.

By 1966, Ireland's music scene had advanced, and at age seventeen, Gallagher hired a drummer and bass player to form the first of two versions of the band Taste. The neo-Cream trio was hailed as one of the best power trios of the day and played mostly Chuck Berry–infused rock and blues. Taste made four albums (two live), and the band established Gallagher as Ireland's ambassador of blues guitar.

In 1970, Taste dissolved for good, but Rory had left his mark. In 1971, he was voted *Melody Maker* magazine's Top International Musician and in 1972 International Guitarist of the Year.

Shortly after Taste, Gallagher began a productive solo career. His singing, writing and guitar playing matured into a mesh of styles including roots rock, hard rock, bluegrass, boogie, country and folk. Between 1971 and 1979, Gallagher released ten albums.

Not surprisingly, his highest-charting album was 1972's *Live in Europe*. After all, the stage was where Rory felt most at home.

HARRY DOHERTY OF ROCK'S BACKPAGES: Rory Gallagher was happiest with a guitar in his hand, playing for and to the crowd. I don't think anybody will ever get to the real man because he kept so much to himself...yet gave so much of himself to all of us.

Gallagher's production tailed off in the 1980s as new music trends challenged rock music's supremacy. From 1980 to 1990 (the year of his final LP), Gallagher released four more albums. Following a successful liver transplant, he contracted a staph infection (MRSA) and passed away on June 14, 1995. An estimated fifteen thousand people lined the streets in Cork, Ireland, when he was laid to rest.

When most musicians shunned Belfast during "The Troubles," Rory performed there regularly. He gave hope to young Irish musicians and fans. His legacy lives on with a lovingly curated website, newly remastered and repackaged music, festivals, memorials and concert DVDs.

MUSICAL INFLUENCES WHO MATTER

Lonnie Donegan, Woody Guthrie, Leadbelly, Big Bill Bronzy, Muddy Waters, Lonnie Mack, Jimmy Reed, Chuck Berry, Jerry Lee Lewis, Albert Collins, B.B. King, Freddie King, Albert King.

PROBABLE CONCERT SETLIST:
B'GINNINGS NIGHT CLUB, NOVEMBER 7, 1974

"Tattoo'd Lady," "Garbage Man," "Cradle Rock," "I Don't Know Why," "Walk on Hot Coals," "A Million Miles Away," "Used to Be," "The Same Thing," "Pistol Slapper Blues," "Too Much Alcohol," "Who's That Coming?" "Bullfrog Blues," "Laundromat," "In Your Town."

JOE COCKER

SINGER, BANDLEADER

JOE COCKER: To know when to put your own stamp on something is very delicate. Sometimes I miss, but once in a while, you can make a tune your own and it becomes something special.

WHY HE MATTERS

Joe Cocker made a career of interpreting the music of others and making their songs his own. The Grammy, Golden Globe and Academy Award–winning artist parlayed his raspy, righteous voice and eccentric stage presence into five decades of international stardom. His career ran the gamut: from the pubs of Sheffield, England, to Max Yasgur's dairy farm. From fallen star to career resurgence.

Cocker played English pubs early in his career and called them the best training ground. In the early 1960s, he formed the band Vance Arnold and the Avengers but soon returned to his day job as a pipe fitter. In 1966, he formed the Grease Band with keyboardist Chris Stainton—a fixture in future Eric Clapton bands. The Grease Band played rock and soul covers in English pubs until 1967, when producer Denny Cordell convinced Cocker and Stainton to relocate to London.

A year later, Cocker catapulted to fame with a reformed Grease Band and recorded their defining album *With a Little Help from My Friends* and the hit single of the same name. Cocker's treatment of the Beatles song was an early example of his interpretative powers. The band changed the original's time signature and received the ultimate compliment from Paul McCartney, who said, "Well, I guess your version is the consummate version."

The Grease Band toured England and played several large American rock festivals, including Woodstock in 1969. Cocker then met guitarist and pianist Leon Russell, who produced the Grease Band's 1969 release *Joe Cocker!* The Beatles gave Cocker permission to record "She Came in Through the Bathroom Window" and "Something" for the same album.

Cocker then joined forces with Russell, who organized and anchored a new band of musicians known as Mad Dogs and Englishman. The rock and soul conglomerate consisted of about forty musicians, crew, wives, girlfriends, children and hangers-on. Drummer Jim Keltner described it as a big, wild party that rolled through forty-eight U.S. cities over a two-month period—then quickly disbanded.

> JOE COCKER: We all lived at Leon's house and ran around in the nude and had some pretty wild times. Having come out of the tour with no money never really bothered me. Back then, the feeling was it was a crime to have money anyway. We were into this trip of stripping ourselves of our worldly goods.

The tour was captured on a self-titled double album followed by a film. But the whirlwind tour left Cocker exhausted. His drinking problem worsened and reduced his once powerful voice to a croaking rasp. He forgot lyrics and showed up late to performances. Nevertheless, he enjoyed success in the 1970s with songs like "High Time We Went," "Midnight Rider" (by Greg Allman) and "You Are So Beautiful" (by Billy Preston).

The 1980s marked a resurgence. He switched record labels and scored a huge hit with the Jennifer Warnes duet "Up Where We Belong." As the theme song for the 1982 film *An Officer and a Gentleman*, it won a Grammy and Academy Award.

More success followed in 1986 and 1987 with "Unchain My Heart" (by Ray Charles) and "You Can Leave Your Hat On" (by Randy Newman). Cocker's version of the latter was used for the striptease scene in the film *9½ Weeks*. Cocker explained, "[In] our version, there's a certain chord that's a bit more commercial and it makes it more danceable." An envious Newman lamented, "Wow, I wish I had put that chord in there. I'd have had myself a hit."

Joe Cocker.

In the 1990s, Cocker and his wife launched several philanthropic foundations. He continued to record and in 2004 released an album of rock, blues and soul favorites titled *Heart and Soul*. Guests included Eric Clapton, Jeff Beck, Jeff "Skunk" Baxter and Steve Lukather of Toto.

Cocker released two more studio albums but then lost his battle with cancer on December 22, 2014. Before Cocker's death, Billy Joel petitioned the Rock & Roll Hall of Fame to induct the singer. As of this writing, they have yet to do so.

MUSICAL INFLUENCES WHO MATTER

Ray Charles, Lonnie Donegan, Aretha Franklin, Staple Singers, Bob Dylan, Muddy Waters, John Lee Hooker, Lightnin' Hopkins.

PROBABLE CONCERT SETLIST: AUDITORIUM THEATRE, SEPTEMBER 18, 1974

"Black Eyed Blues," "Delta Lady," "With a Little Help from My Friends," "High Time We Went," "Hitchcock Railway," "I Get Mad," "I Got to Wait," "Pardon Me Sir," "When I Get the Feelin'," "You Are So Beautiful."

LEON RUSSELL

PIANIST, GUITARIST, SINGER, SONGWRITER, ARRANGER, SESSION PLAYER, PRODUCER

HAL BLAINE: When he sat down at the piano, he turned the record business upside down. Every producer wanted Leon Russell. He brought savage solos to our sessions and added a key element to our hit record formula.

WHY HE MATTERS

By itself, Russell's drawl-infused, raspy and nasal-toned singing would not predict future greatness. But when layered over powerful left-hand piano rhythms, arpeggios and delicate classical flourishes, something transformative resulted.

Leon Russell began classical piano lessons at the age of four, despite being born with an injury that left his right hand weakened. There were other hardships early in his life. At age fourteen, Leon was playing in Oklahoma nightclubs with J.J. Cale, future members of Bob Dylan's band and Jerry Lee Lewis.

Around 1959, he headed for Los Angeles to study guitar with the legendary James Burton and became a member of an elite clan of studio musicians dubbed the "Wrecking Crew." As a 1960s studio musician, Russell contributed to hit songs by many stars of the day, including Jan and Dean, Aretha Franklin, Frank Sinatra, the Beach Boys, the Byrds, Paul Revere and the Raiders, Gary Lewis and the Playboys, Wayne Newton and others.

Leon Russell.

By the late 1960s, he had ventured out of the shadows and began writing and recording his own music. As an entrepreneur, he co-founded recording label Shelter Records and built a studio in a converted Tulsa church. He continued his session role by playing with legendary musicians, including rock and soul band Delaney and Bonnie. Eric Clapton famously tapped Russell and friends for his first solo album.

About this time, Russell was finding his own reputation as a bandleader by organizing and anchoring Joe Cocker's legendary Mad Dogs and Englishmen tour. He also played bandleader in rock's first major charity event, The Concert for Bangladesh.

Throughout the 1970s, Russell released his own albums, jumpstarted the career of blues guitarist Freddie King, toured with the Rolling Stones and wrote many songs that became hits for others. "Song for You" won a Grammy for Ray Charles, and "The Masquerade" became a Top 10 hit for jazz guitarist/singer George Benson.

Russell also delved into his country roots. He released several albums under the name Hank Wilson and recorded and toured with Willie Nelson. But when music trends changed, he went from filling arenas to a forgotten man.

In 2008, serendipity struck. On a British talk show, Elton John mentioned Russell as one of the singer-songwriters shamefully forgotten. He confessed that Russell was his idol and the musician he most wanted to play and sing like.

LEON RUSSELL: I was lying in bed watching *As the World Turns* when [Elton] called me from Africa—on his elephant—and asked if I'd like to make a record with him.

In 2010, a John and Russell studio collaboration resulted in *The Union*. The album skyrocketed to no. 3 on the U.S. charts and sold well in other countries. Cameron Crowe's moving documentary about the making of the album was released in 2011.

Russell's career received the ultimate validation with inductions into the Rock & Roll Hall of Fame and Country Music Songwriters Hall of Fame.

In an interview with *Keyboard* magazine, Russell was asked about the proudest moments in his career. Russell responded, "I guess that I'm still alive, and that I've never sold anybody a bad car." Typically humble for someone who spent years giving more than he took.

On November 13, 2016, the man billed as the "Master of Space and Time" passed away at his home in Nashville, Tennessee. He was seventy-four years old.

MUSICAL INFLUENCES WHO MATTER

Errol Garner, Jerry Lee Lewis, Huey "Piano" Smith, Ray Charles, Allen Toussaint, Professor Longhair, James Burton, J.J. Cale, Hank Williams, Ronnie Hawkins, Doc Pomus, Hoagy Carmichael, Bob Dylan, the Beatles, the Rolling Stones.

PROBABLE CONCERT SETLIST:
CHICAGO STADIUM, MARCH 23, 1973

"Blues Power," "Shoot Out on the Plantation," "Dixie Lullaby," "Roller Derby," "Roll Away the Stone," "It's Been a Long Time Baby," "Great Day," "Alcatraz," "Crystal Closet Queen," "Prince of Peace," "Sweet Emily," "Stranger in a Strange Land," "Out in the Woods," "Sweeping Through the City," "Jumpin' Jack Flash," "Of Thee I Sing," "Delta Lady," "It's All Over," "Now Baby Blue."

Pete Townshend.

THE WHO

FORMED 1964

BAND MEMBERS WHO MATTER

Pete Townshend (lead guitar, vocals, keyboards), Roger Daltrey (vocals, harmonica, guitar), John Entwistle (bass, French horn, vocals), Keith Moon (drums).

PARKE PUTERBAUGH/ROCK & ROLL HALL OF FAME: With the Beatles and the Rolling Stones, the Who round out a triumvirate of British bands that revolutionized rock 'n' roll. The members of the Who never simply played rock 'n' roll, they attacked it—along with their instruments.

WHY THEY MATTER

The kids were alright: rebellious and irreverent, polished and literate and complex and theatrical. They originated the rock opera concept, introduced the world to high-energy live performances and were the first serious rock band to incorporate synthesizers. Commercially, The Who racked up an impressive number of high-charting singles and albums. Many remain enduring masterworks.

How loud were they in concert? According to *Guinness World Records*, on May 31,1976, their sound measured 126 decibels at 100 feet, a record that lasted ten years! But members of the band paid the price.

Pete Townshend, John Entwistle and Roger Daltrey all grew up in Acton, London, and attended the same county grammar school. Townshend's parents encouraged their son to pursue his rock 'n' roll dream inspired by the 1956 movie, *Rock Around the Clock*. Entwistle received formal music training and played French horn in a youth orchestra before finding work in a British tax office. Daltrey was an intelligent young man with an attitude. He was expelled from school and took day work in a sheet metal factory and made guitars for his band, the Detours.

In late 1963, Entwistle and Townshend joined Daltrey in the Detours. At an impromptu audition, they were stunned by a bloke who played drums with such unrestraint that his kit needed anchoring. That wild man was Keith Moon, and the legendary Who lineup was in place from 1964 until Moon's death in September 1978.

Early on, they found an audience in the mods, a 1960s English youth subculture that became the subject of the Who's 1973 concept album *Quadrophenia* and the movie that followed.

A key moment for the quartet arrived in 1964 at the Railway Tavern in London. Townshend accidentally damaged his guitar's headstock against the venue's low ceiling. Out of frustration, he smashed what was left of his instrument. As a result, their next concert drew a large audience, and Moon obliged by wrecking his drum kit. Their reputation for instrument demolition had begun.

With the 1965 release of their breakthrough song "My Generation," the band solidified their role as spokesmen for a frustrated generation. Radio Caroline, a pirate radio station portrayed in the 2009 film *Pirate Radio*, helped bring early Who music to the British underground.

The band's reputation as one rock's greatest live acts (listen to *Live at Leeds*) was honed over several years of endless touring needed to offset lost royalties from lawsuits with the band's first producer. Unfortunately, this wasn't the only revenue screwing the band experienced.

Musically, the Who had no weak links. Pete Townshend's trademarks were the innovative use of power chords, controlled feedback, the blending of electric and acoustic guitars and clever chord inversions. So were his stage theatrics: windmill strumming, leaping and sliding across the stage on his knees.

At the age of twenty-two, Townshend learned keyboards, further changing the trajectory of the Who's music. He developed a reputation as one of rock's most literate and articulate members, and his vocals were the perfect counter to Daltrey's.

Roger Daltrey.

Pete Townshend (*left*) and Keith Moon.

Keith Moon.

ALICE COOPER: Pete's the best stage guitarist I've ever seen—the best showman, conveying the pure spirit of rock and roll. And he's still up there with his fingers bleeding to this day.

The Who's real lead instrument was not guitar but rather Keith Moon's drums, John Entwistle's bass and Roger Daltrey's voice. Keith Moon was a tour de force percussionist with one the most flamboyant and unorthodox approaches to drumming. If there was any musical space unclaimed by the others, he filled it. Nicknamed "Moon the Loon," Keith took delight in his hedonistic lifestyle. It eventually did him in, and the Who was never the same. Ex-Faces drummer Kenney Jones assumed Moon's duties from 1978 to 1988. But Moon's energy was noticeably missing.

John Entwistle played bass like a lead guitar. A *Musician* magazine poll voted him "Bassist of the Millennium." Nicknamed "The Ox" and

"Thunderfingers," Entwistle was as nimble on bass as a banjo picker. He produced a thunderous upper register sound as he experimented with scales, active bass electronics and amplification. As a formally trained musician, his ability to arrange brass instruments made him the band's most talented musician. Despite a limited number of writing credits, he revealed a wry and dark sense of humor in the songs "My Wife," "Boris the Spider" and "Fiddle About."

BILL WYMAN: Entwistle was the quietest man in private but the loudest man onstage.

Roger Daltrey was made for rock stardom with his good looks, long golden curls and tanned chest. In Ken Russell's 1975 movie *Tommy*, he brilliantly transformed himself into Townshend's deaf, dumb and blind boy.

On stage, Daltrey had many performing trademarks: fringed leather jackets, marching in place and throwing his corded microphone like a rodeo cowboy. And despite his small stature, he possessed a distinct muscular roar heard on such songs as "We Won't Get Fooled Again," "I'm Free," "Love Reign O'er Me" and "Baba O'Riley." More importantly, his voice reinforced the mood behind Townshend's lyrics.

On the eve of a tour in June 2002, the Who suffered another irreparable blow when John Entwistle died of a heart attack in his Las Vegas hotel

Left to right: Roger Daltrey, John Entwistle, Keith Moon and Pete Townshend.

room. But Townshend and Daltrey agreed to carry on recording, performing and touring separately and with each other.

In 2019, the Who released their twelfth studio album, simply titled *Who*. Long live rock, be it dead or alive.

MUSICAL INFLUENCES WHO MATTER

Jimmy Reed, Eddie Cochran, Georgie Fame, James Brown, Jackie Wilson, Mose Allison, John Lee Hooker, Ray Charles, Charlie Parker, Chet Atkins, Duane Eddy, Gene Krupa, Buddy Rich.

PROBABLE CONCERT SETLIST:
CHICAGO STADIUM, DECEMBER 4, 1975

"I Can't Explain," "Substitute," "Squeeze Box," "Baba O'Riley," "My Wife," "Behind Blue Eyes," "Dreaming from the Waist," "Magic Bus," "Amazing Journey," "Sparks," "The Acid Queen," "Fiddle About," "Pinball Wizard," "I'm Free," "Tommy's Holiday Camp," "We're Not Gonna Take It," "See Me, Feel Me," "Summertime Blues," "My Generation," "Join Together," "My Generation Blues," "Road Runner," "Won't Get Fooled Again," "Drowned."

THE KINKS

FORMED 1963

BAND MEMBERS WHO MATTER

Ray Davies (lead vocals, songwriter, piano, rhythm guitar), Dave Davies (lead guitar, vocals), Peter Quaife (bass, backing vocals), Mick Avory (drums).

ROLLING STONE RECORD GUIDE: There had never been a rock 'n' roll sound like the one introduced by the Kinks on their first hit. With one simple riff, Dave Davies virtually invented power-chord rock.

WHY THEY MATTER

It was never easy being the Kinks: sibling rivalry, creative differences, sleazy management, frozen royalties and a four-year U.S. ban. Despite it all, the Kinks were one of the most important and commercially successful British invasion bands.

Brothers Ray and Dave Davies were only sixteen and thirteen, respectively, when their parents signed their first music contract as members of the Ravens. With bass-playing school chum Peter Quaife and jazz drummer Mick Avory rounding out the quartet, the Ravens became the Kinks. The name was intended to raise eyebrows.

Their first two singles fell flat, but the third was a game-changer. "You Really Got Me" was a Mose Allison–inspired tune written on piano by Ray

Davies. Yet it was brother Dave's immortal power chords that made history. Ramones drummer Marky Ramone proclaimed, "It was the first punk rock guitar sound."

Along with Ray's sexually charged delivery and lyrics, the 1964 hit featured one of the greatest opening riffs ever recorded and paved the way for garage, punk and metal in just two minutes and twenty seconds.

DAVE DAVIES: I got a razor blade and cut around the cone [of my speaker] so it was all shredded but still intact. I felt like an inventor.

Over the next two years, the quartet recorded more epic rockers: "All Day and All of the Night," "Till the End of the Day," "Set Me Free" and "Who'll Be the Next in Line." But they weren't limited by formulaic garage rock thanks to lead singer Ray Davies—a powerful tunesmith who earned a reputation as the quintessential chronicler of English life.

From 1965 to 1969, the Kinks were banned from performing in the United States due to an unresolved union dispute. As a result, Davies took refuge in his English roots and used pop songs as social essays that chronicled the little absurdities and aspirations of English life.

The hits continued with wistful ballads like "Tired of Waiting for You," "Sunny Afternoon," "Well Respected Man," "Waterloo Sunset" and "Dedicated Follower of Fashion." All featured a world-weary singing style that was more reserved than earlier tunes.

Around 1968, the band shifted from singles to concept albums beginning with *The Kinks Are the Village Green Preservation Society*. Despite critical acclaim, it was a modest commercial success. A year later, they released *Arthur (Or the Decline and Fall of the British Empire)*. The album contained themes about the vanishing of traditional English life and glory. The single "Victoria" made England's Top 40, but the U.S. market didn't understand the subject matter.

In 1969, original member Peter Quaife departed. He had long felt left out of the creative process and grew tired of band member bickering. But Quaife later admitted, "Ray Davies—pain in the ass that he could be—was a damn good songwriter!" Quaife was replaced on bass by John Dalton.

With keyboardist John Gosling rounding out the revised lineup, the Kinks entered a new period of commercial success. The 1970 album *Lola Versus Powerman* and *The Moneygoround Part One* demonstrated Ray's sardonic humor and social satire with the singles "Lola" (about a transvestite encounter) and "Apeman" (a swipe at modern living).

Ray Davies.

A year later, they released *Muswell Hillbillies* in reference to the North London suburb where Ray and Dave grew up. The LP blended English middle-class themes with strong elements of country and music hall influences. But their traditional fan base was not evolving, and their popularity waned over the next six years.

In 1977, the Kinks signed to Arista Records and experienced a resurgence by returning to traditional rock. Lead guitarist Dave Davies was particularly happy. One of their best-selling albums was *One for the Road* (also on video), released in 1980.

With the help of MTV, the nostalgic dance hall tune "Come Dancing" was the band's highest-charting Billboard and Cash Box single since the mid-1960s.

In 1984, original band member Mick Avory left. The Kinks would never crack the Top 40 again. In 1990—their first year of eligibility—the Kinks were inducted into the Rock & Roll Hall of Fame and in 2005 joined the U.K. Music Hall of Fame. Ray Davies remarked, "The Kinks have always been outsiders. I'm an outsider. To be accepted is unique for us."

MUSICAL INFLUENCES WHO MATTER

The Ventures, the Shadows, Duane Eddy, Bo Diddley, Lonnie Donegan, Slim Harpo, Chuck Berry, Little Richard, Carl Perkins, Otis Redding, the Beatles, Leadbelly, Lightning Hopkins, Muddy Waters, Eddie Cochran, Big Bill Broonzy, Buddy Rich, Art Blakey, Philly Jo Jones, Joe Morello, Mose Allison, Cole Porter, Irving Berlin.

PROBABLE CONCERT SETLIST:
AUDITORIUM THEATRE, APRIL 16, 1974

"Victoria," "One of the Survivors," "Celluloid Heroes," "Money Talks," "You Really Got Me," "All Day and All of the Night," "Sunny Afternoon," "Lola," "Here Comes Yet Another Day," "Here Comes Flash," "Mr. Wonderful," "Alcohol," "Skin and Bone," "Dem Bones," "Good Golly, Miss Molly."

THE MOODY BLUES

FORMED 1964

BAND MEMBERS WHO MATTER

Denny Laine (guitar, vocals), Justin Hayward (guitar, vocals), John Lodge (bass, vocals), Mike Pinder (keyboards, including Mellotron, vocals), Ray Thomas (flute, harmonica, percussion, vocals), Graeme Edge (drums).

> **GRAEME EDGE:** We were all convinced that rock music was only a short-term thing and that we'd be working in the mines in a few short years. We were so broke and miserable playing music we didn't like, so why not be miserable and broke playing music that we liked?

WHY THEY MATTER

In 1964, a band from Birmingham, England, scored a no. 1 hit with their cover of "Go Now." Fame came quickly for the Moody Blues, but so did their descent. Tired of being broke and heading nowhere musically, original members Denny Laine and Clint Warwick departed. Justin Hayward and John Lodge filled their slots.

It was time to rethink the band's direction. According to Hayward, the Moodys' moment of clarity arrived when a man knocked on their dressing room door and told them they were the worst rhythm 'n' blues band he'd ever seen. They agreed.

Justin Hayward.

Around 1967, they began working on their own material and launched their own record label to control the creative process. Their musical makeover was a success beginning with the 1967 LP *Days of Future Passed*. It was a groundbreaking rock concept album that spawned the timeless classics "Nights in White Satin" and "Tuesday Afternoon."

The Moody Blues had found their sound: an orchestrated fusion of pop, folk and psychedelic music supplemented with four-part vocals, memorable melodies and profound lyrics. Some labeled it "symphonic pop."

The foundation for their new sound was provided by keyboardist Mike Pinder and his mellotron. The odd-looking organ-like instrument used prerecorded tape loops to produce orchestrated sounds.

MIKE PINDER: I will never forget seeing and playing [it] for the first time. This was my first "man on the moon" event. I knew that my life had led to this moment, the portent to the future. The instrument felt like an old friend.

Until his departure, Pinder was responsible for much of the Moody Blues' conceptual direction and symphonic sound arrangements. From 1967 through 1972, the band entered its classic album phase. They made seven highly successful LPs that spawned a slew of rock radio classics such as "Ride My See-Saw," "Question" and "Legend of a Mind." They sold out auditoriums and broke attendance records. With no obvious frontman, flautist Ray Thomas referred to the group as a "Communist band run with capitalistic intentions." In America, the band's music was reaching a college-educated fan base looking for mind-expanding music and meaning.

JUSTIN HAYWARD: We had all these people at our feet asking, "What is the word?" "What is the answer?" They treated us like gurus, and it was scary.

In 1972, the Moodys released *Seventh Sojourn*, the last of their seven classic albums. It topped the charts in the United States. The John Lodge single "I'm Just a Singer in a Rock and Roll Band" was a not-so-subtle message for misguided fans. A year of touring followed. The band was road weary, and the financial cost of touring a band like the Moodys was draining.

A five-year hiatus ensued, and during that time, Decca Records deemed it necessary to rekindle band interest by releasing old material. When keyboardist Patrick Moraz (ex-Yes) replaced Mike Pinder in 1978, the band

Mike Pinder.

returned to the studio and released *Long Distance Voyager*. It topped the charts in the United States. However, nothing that followed would match the band's glory years. Moraz departed in 1991. The split wasn't amicable.

Members Justin Hayward, John Lodge, Ray Thomas and Graeme Edge carried on, but in 2002, Thomas retired. He passed away just prior to the band's Rock & Roll Hall of Fame induction in 2018. Drummer Graeme Edge retired in 2018, marking the unofficial end of the touring band. He passed away in late 2021. Heading into 2024, John Lodge and Justin Hayward continued to tour individually and release material celebrating the pioneers of symphonic pop.

MUSICAL INFLUENCES WHO MATTER

Freddie Bell and the Bellboys, Gene Vincent and the Bluecaps, Jerry Lee Lewis, Little Richard, Chuck Berry, Elvis Presley, Buddy Holly, Cliff Richard, Eric Clapton, James Brown, Duke Ellington.

PROBABLE CONCERT SETLIST:
CHICAGO STADIUM, OCTOBER 30, 1973

"Higher and Higher," "Out and In," "The Story in Your Eyes," "One More Time to Live," "Tuesday Afternoon," "Legend of a Mind," "Watching and Waiting," "Eternity Road," "Melancholy Man," "Are You Sitting Comfortably?" "The Dream," "Have You Heard (Part 1)," "The Voyage," "Have You Heard (Part 2)," "Nights in White Satin," "I'm Just a Singer (In a Rock and Roll Band)," "Question," "Ride My See-Saw."

Steve Winwood.

TRAFFIC

FORMED 1967

BAND MEMBERS WHO MATTER

Steve Winwood (keyboards, guitar, bass, vocals), Chris Wood (reed instruments, organ, vocals), Jim Capaldi (drums, percussion, vocals), Dave Mason (guitar, sitar, mellotron, vocals).

> STEVE WINWOOD: Traffic for me was all about mixing jazz, folk, ethnic music, rock and rhythm 'n' blues. We wanted to forge our own music by trying to combine those different elements.

WHY THEY MATTER

Traffic was one of the most musically adventurous and distinct-sounding bands of the late 1960s and early 1970s. The core consisted of Steve Winwood, Jim Capaldi and Chris Wood. Co-founder Dave Mason made his mark on the band's first two albums and would reappear at times. Traffic fluctuated from three to seven members, which altered their sound and dictated their stage capabilities.

The music focused on mood and texture with a priority placed on haunting vocals, keyboards, reed instruments and exotic rhythms. Guitar parts served a more a compositional role, although Winwood occasionally unleashed his chops.

The idea for Traffic took root in a Birmingham (England) bar where Winwood, Capaldi, Wood and Mason shared ideas and jammed. With financial backing from Island Records founder Chris Blackwell, the four formed Traffic.

The quartet began as a hippie-like musical cooperative. They lived communally and practiced in a secluded stone cottage with few modern conveniences. Early Traffic scored three Top 10 songs in the United Kingdom. Their 1967 debut LP *Mr. Fantasy* (also released as *Heaven Is in Your Mind*) was a mix of rock jams, English dance hall music and trippy pop songs.

But musical differences surfaced between Mason and the others. While Mason had the ability to write likeable pop songs, Winwood preferred a more collaborative approach that favored jazz-like improvisation.

DAVE MASON: "[Hole in My] Shoe" was the first song I ever wrote. I mean...that stuff I did back then—when I listen to it—I cringe. But writing comes out of living. That song was the beginning of the end for me as far as the other three guys were concerned.

Mason temporarily departed, and Traffic toured the United States as a trio. His absence was felt musically and instrumentally. A reconciliation brought Mason back to the studio, where he contributed several songs to the band's second album, simply titled *Traffic*. Released in late 1968, the album got America's attention.

Mason again departed. In mid-1969, Winwood went on to join guitarist Eric Clapton, drummer Ginger Baker and bassist Ric Grech in the short-lived supergroup Blind Faith.

After Blind Faith ended, Winwood went to work on a solo album with the help of former Traffic bandmates Capaldi and Wood. The sessions were so productive that the trio reformed Traffic. The result was *John Barleycorn Must Die*, released in 1970. The grooves were filled with old English folk– and jazz-derived riffs. In the United States, the LP achieved gold sales certification, and songs like "Glad," "Freedom Rider" and "John Barleycorn" became rock radio staples.

In anticipation of another tour, Traffic expanded to seven members, and Dave Mason returned for a smattering of U.K. shows. The result was *Welcome to the Canteen*, a live album credited to each member of the touring band. Traffic had now found its audience in America.

Chris Wood.

JIM CAPALDI: We were looked on as being an underground group like the Dead or Airplane because we played in those early acid days when it was all happening in California.

The same musicians—excluding Mason—came together in late 1971 for one of Traffic's most heralded studio albums: *The Low Spark of High Heeled Boys*. It was Traffic's only platinum-selling album and featured an eye-catching six-sided album jacket. But as the band was hitting its stride, Steve Winwood was sidelined with a life-changing case of peritonitis.

Once Winwood recovered, he, Capaldi and Wood recorded 1973's *Shoot Out at the Fantasy Factory*—another U.S. Top 10 album. A year later, *When the Eagle Flies* became Traffic's fourth-straight Top 10 album and the first since *John Barleycorn* to chart in the United Kingdom. It was the final album that Winwood, Capaldi and Wood worked on together. In 2004, the original four were inducted into the Rock & Roll Hall of Fame.

MUSICAL INFLUENCES WHO MATTER

The Beatles, Elvis Presley, Bob Dylan, Booker T. & the M.G.'s, J.S. Bach, Oscar Brown, Small Faces, the Doors, Jimi Hendrix, Cream, Jefferson Airplane, Grateful Dead, Little Richard, Fats Domino, Ray Charles, Charles Mingus, Chico Hamilton, Charlie Parker, Miles Davis, Jimmy Smith, Curtis Mayfield, T-Bone Walker, Eddie Condon, Hank Marvin, the Ventures, the Hunters, Rhett Stoller.

PROBABLE CONCERT SETLIST:
AUDITORIUM THEATRE, OCTOBER 27, 1974

"Shoot Out at the Fantasy Factory," "Empty Pages," "Graveyard People," "Pearly Queen," "Who Knows What Tomorrow May Bring," "Love," "Something New," "Walking in the Wind," "John Barleycorn," "Forty Thousand Headmen," "When the Eagle Flies," "Dream Gerrard," "The Low Spark of High-Heeled Boys."

DAVE MASON

SINGER, SONGWRITER, GUITAR, BASS, COMPOSER

MICK FLEETWOOD: He's been here, there and everywhere, but he's always found a way of prevailing.

WHY HE MATTERS

Years ago, writer Bill DeYoung wrote in *Goldmine* magazine: "[Dave Mason] is a rock 'n' roll survivor. He's had more life experiences than Forrest Gump. Dave Mason eagerly reached into [his] box of chocolates never quite knowing what he was going to get."

Dave Mason has had many sweet moments in his career. He was a founding member of the landmark band Traffic and, as such, a member of the Rock & Roll Hall of Fame. His lengthy and prolific solo career is awash with timeless classics like "Feelin' Alright?," "Only You Know and I Know," "World of Changes," "Look at You Look at Me," "We Just Disagree," "Show Me Some Affection," "The Lonely One" and "Shouldn't Have Took More Than You Gave."

And as Mick Fleetwood said, he's been everywhere. Mason worked with Jimi Hendrix; the Rolling Stones; Delaney and Bonnie; Eric Clapton; George Harrison; Paul McCartney; Fleetwood Mac; Crosby, Stills and Nash; Bob Dylan; Joe Walsh; Dave Brubeck; Stevie Wonder; Steve Cropper; and Joe Bonamassa. Out of breath yet?

Dave Mason.

Born on May 10, 1946, in Worcester, England, Mason developed an interest in guitar when a family trip brought him to America. Music on American radio caught the introverted lad's ear. Instrumental music was his original interest. At age sixteen, he made his debut by recording an instrumental piece at a YMCA that was sold through a local record shop.

Mason then took up singing in order to get local bookings. He studied music and played in bands that included future Traffic bandmates. He was a road manager for the Spencer Davis Group with which Steve Winwood sang and played keyboards. In 1967, he co-founded the band Traffic.

Mason wrote or co-wrote five songs on each of Traffic's first two albums, including his signature song "Feelin' Alright," a classic famously covered by Joe Cocker and dozens of others. But his in-and-out time with Traffic was stormy. Nevertheless, Mason looks back on the experience positively. In 2023, he told co-hosts Jim Summaria and Mark Plotnick of *That Classic Rock Show*, "Traffic gave me an opportunity for a music career and doing what I loved."

Over the next few years, Mason began a solo career while still working in a band context. He joined the rock 'n' soul band Delaney and Bonnie, played with Eric Clapton in an early version of Derek and the Dominoes, contributed to George Harrison's renowned LP *All Things Must Pass* and recorded with friend Cass Elliot.

Wanting something of his own, Mason signed with Blue Thumb Records and in 1970 released his debut LP *Alone Together*. The album featured top-drawer session players and demonstrated Mason's maturing talent as a songwriter, singer and guitarist. Despite its success, Mason felt his vocal performance needed work. He set a very high bar for himself. He told Jim Summaria and Mark Plotnick that his high bar was Sam Cooke, Marvin Gaye and Mahalia Jackson.

After *Alone Together*, Mason ran into myriad managerial, contractual and financial setbacks that nearly brought him to his knees. But Dave Mason was a survivor.

DAVE MASON: I'm not interested in the victim mentality....As for me, if I'd have known better, I'd have done better. But I'd like to thank all the people that [screwed] me because it's been quite an education.

The multifaceted musician dealt with adversity the only way he knew how: by writing more songs, singing, playing guitar, recording new music, building a music studio, collaborating and touring. He reached into his box of chocolates and worked on a Miller Beer commercial and Patrick Swayze movie. He gave back via philanthropic causes.

Dave has never been shy about his music industry opinions—an industry that has struggled with Dave Mason's niche.

> **DAVE MASON:** I'm not a blues artist. I'm not a pop artist. I'm not a ballad guy. I'm not a rock 'n' roll guy. I'm not a jazz guy. I'm all of these...so there's no set tag you can put on me musically....It's about the song, and each song requires a different approach.

Dave Mason continues to do what Dave Mason does. In 2018, he and Rock Hall of Famer Steve Cropper released a live CD titled *4Real Rock & Soul Revue*. In 2020, Mason celebrated the fiftieth anniversary of his debut solo album with the album *Alone Together Again*. He then collaborated with guitar great Joe Bonamassa to breathe new life into the classic 1967 Traffic song "Dear Mr. Fantasy."

Mason still performs over one hundred shows a year. His 2023 Endangered Species tour was a tongue-in-cheek reference to his vanishing kind. In 2024, Dave Mason hit the road again with his Traffic Jam tour. His goal is to keep the music of Traffic, Dave Mason and others alive. Dave Mason is a survivor!

MUSICAL INFLUENCES WHO MATTER

Hank Marvin and the Shadows, Outlaws (not the southern rock band), the Ventures, the Hunters, the Tornados, George Benson, Elmore James, Buddy Guy, B.B. King, Albert King, Freddie King, Eddie Cochran, Little Richard, Gene Vincent and the Blue Caps, Carl Perkins, Dorsey Burnette, Johnny and the Hurricanes, Duane Eddy, Jerry Lee Lewis, Buddy Holly.

PROBABLE CONCERT SETLIST: ARIE CROWN THEATER, NOVEMBER 25, 1975

"Feelin' Alright?," "Waitin' on You," "Show Me Some Affection," "Split Coconut," "World in Changes," "Every Woman," "Look at You Look at Me," "Headkeeper," "Only You Know and I Know," "All Along the Watchtower," "Gimme Some Lovin'," "Bring It on Home to Me," "Baby...Please."

BLACK SABBATH

FORMED 1969

BAND MEMBERS WHO MATTER

Ozzy Osbourne (lead vocals), Tony Iommi (guitar), Geezer Butler (bass), Bill Ward (drums).

> **DAVE NAVARRO:** Black Sabbath are the Beatles of heavy metal. Anybody who is serious about metal will tell you it all comes down to Sabbath.

WHY THEY MATTER

Black Sabbath was the touchstone that evolved heavy blues rock into heavy metal rock, a genre that married despair, distortion-heavy riffs and sledgehammer drumming played at high volume levels. When Metallica's James Hetfield recalled the first time he heard the song "Black Sabbath," he said, "It scared the shit out of me. It was beyond heavy."

But initially, the band had detractors. In *Rolling Stone* magazine's *1985 Record Guide*, the reviewer assigned a one-star rating to all eleven Sabbath albums between 1970 and 1981. Ouch!

Guess who got the last laugh? Today, the band is universally acknowledged as the godfather of heavy metal rock—a genre with influence decades beyond the band's debut.

Ozzy Osbourne.

MUSICIAN MAGAZINE: They brought rock and roll into the age of Stephen King by pulling up its pagan roots for all to see.

To date, Sabbath has sold an estimated seventy-plus million albums worldwide, and Ozzy (born John Michael Osbourne) is a household name.

Several factors shaped the band's pioneering sound—not the least being their birthplace. Original members grew up in a poor district of Birmingham, England, an industrial town that carried the physical and emotional scars of World War II bombing by the Nazis. It was a bleak environment.

Ozzy had a difficult childhood. He suffered from learning disabilities and was taunted by classmates. The Beatles inspired the future "Prince of Darkness" to escape his troubles and pursue a singing career. He was also inspired by soul music.

Anthony Frank "Tony" Iommi lost two fingertips in a factory accident. He fashioned thimble-like extensions for his damaged fretting fingers. He accommodated his handicap further by tuning his guitar strings down to make them less taut and subsequently lower in pitch. By messing around with the flatted fifth, the guitarist pioneered distorted riffs that were thick and ominous sounding.

Geezer Butler dropped his bass tuning to match Iommi's tuning and experimented with effects pedals. As the band's primary wordsmith, his fascination with black arts, science fiction and global annihilation helped shape Sabbath's lyrics.

And finally, William Thomas "Bill" Ward's drumming barrage differed greatly from the jazz and big band drummers he admired.

BILL WARD: In order to support Tony and Geezer, I needed to play heavy, hard and loud. They were turning out some of the most intense, unbelievable riffs and I went where I needed to go to support them.

The muffled mixes of early Sabbath recordings also shaped Sabbath's sludgy sound. Eventually, critics warmed up to the band's music and with the support of heavy touring, their first five albums achieved platinum sales status. With the arrival of their sixth album, *Sabotage*, the band had seemingly reached its peak. One year later, the demons of rock 'n' roll came home to roost. The band was plagued by creative disputes, drugs and alcohol and lawsuits from parents.

Ozzy briefly departed in 1977 but was dismissed for good in 1979. He was replaced by Rainbow singer Ronnie James Dio. Ironically, it was

Right: Tony Iommi.

Opposite, left: Bill Ward.

Opposite, right: Geezer Butler.

Ozzy's future wife, Sharon, who recommended Dio. Ronnie could belt out a song with the best of them, and two worthy Sabbath albums resulted: 1980's *Heaven and Hell* and 1981's *Mob Rules*. But things were never the same.

Sabbath encountered more personality conflicts. Bill Ward left in 1980, only to return in 1983. Many players continued to shuffle in and out, with Iommi being the only constant over time.

Under Sharon Osbourne's management and loving care, Ozzy turned his name into a money-making brand that began with two powerful solo albums: *Blizzard of Oz* and *Diary of a Madman*.

The four originals reunited briefly in 1992 and 1997. A 2001 reunion minus Bill Ward (contract dispute) yielded the LP simply titled *13*. Producer Rick Rubin was driven to return Sabbath to its early sound, and the result was the band's first no. 1 album on the Billboard 200. Although *13* topped the charts in several other countries, it was the band's final studio effort.

The originals—again without Ward—had one more live album in them. *The End* captured them performing before their hometown fans in 2017.

There's no denying Black Sabbath's immeasurable influence on metal bands like Metallica, Motörhead, Black Flag, Anthrax, Pantera, Dokken, Sepultura, Rollins Band, Danzig and many others.

Osbourne, Iommi, Butler and Ward were inducted into the U.K. Music Hall of Fame in 2005 and the Rock & Roll Hall of Fame in 2006. In 2019, Black Sabbath received a Grammy Lifetime Achievement Award.

MUSICAL INFLUENCES WHO MATTER

The Beatles, Hank Marvin and the Shadows, Jimi Hendrix, Blue Cheer, Django Reinhardt, Vanilla Fudge, Cream, Yardbirds, Sam and Dave, Deep Purple, Led Zeppelin, Iron Butterfly, the Who, Muddy Waters, John Mayall's Bluesbreakers, Frank Zappa, Jack Bruce, Buddy Rich, Gene Krupa, Dizzy Gillespie.

PROBABLE CONCERT SETLIST:
INTERNATIONAL AMPHITHEATER, FEBRUARY 11, 1974

"Tomorrow's Dream," "Sweet Leaf," "Killing Yourself to Live," "Snowblind," "Sabbra Cadabra," "Sometimes I'm Happy," "Supernaut," "Iron Man," "Don't Start (Too Late)," "Black Sabbath," "Embryo," "Children of the Grave," "War Pigs," "Paranoid."

UFO

FORMED 1969

BAND MEMBERS WHO MATTER

Phil Mogg (lead vocals), Andy Parker (drums), Pete Way (bass), Paul Raymond (keyboards, rhythm guitar, vocals), Michael Schenker (guitar), Paul Chapman (guitar).

> **PHIL MOGG:** I don't think we ever thought of ourselves as rock stars. We were just a bunch of blokes playing in a band and getting reasonably successful. An audience can normally sniff you out if you've gone fake.

WHY THEY MATTER

Extraterrestrials? Hardly…but if life on other planets can rock like these Brits did, Earth welcomes you! The history of UFO is long and tumultuous with plenty of rock 'n' roll shenanigans. And through it all has been co-founder and lead vocalist Phil Mogg.

Built around some of the most lethal guitar hooks, testosterone-infused vocals and jackhammer-like bass and drum accompaniments on earth, UFO made its name with rock anthems like "Rock Bottom," "Lights Out," "Only You Can Rock Me," "Doctor Doctor," "Too Hot to Handle," "Hot 'n' Ready" and "We Belong to the Night."

The band's origins trace back to original members Pete Way and Mick Bolton in a trio called Boyfriends. They were joined by Phil Mogg, who shunned his parents' advice to get a respectable job. The three added a drummer whose smelly feet—among other things—made for a short stint. With new drummer Andy Parker, the band settled on UFO—the name of a London music nightclub.

Musically, the teenage quartet began as a progressive space and blues-rock outfit whose music connected in Japan and Germany. Their first three albums barely registered beyond these markets. But key moments change fortunes.

In July 1973, then guitarist Bernie Marsden misplaced his passport prior to a German gig. As showtime neared, UFO was without a guitarist. As fate would have it, the Scorpions were opening and lent their blond guitar wunderkind named Michael Schenker.

The young German knew little English, but his ability on guitar was all anyone needed. Over the next five years, the Schenker era marked a new direction for UFO's music. With the success and popularity that followed, so did a period of chronic tension between Schenker and his British bandmates. Cultural differences and a language barrier played a role. Without exception, band members were in awe of his musicianship and have publicly acknowledged his crucial role in UFO's success.

> **PAUL RAYMOND:** He's one of the most technically brilliant players I've ever seen. But the problems with Michael began when he started to believe what others were saying about how fantastic he was.

The band's debut on a major label (Chrysalis) was the 1974 LP *Phenomenon*. It featured classic UFO songs like "Doctor Doctor" and "Rock Bottom." *Rolling Stone* magazine predicted that UFO would become very big in a very short time. They proved the magazine accurate.

More personnel changes followed. Paul Raymond of Savoy Brown joined when UFO desired a new keyboard player who could double on guitar. And respected Welsh guitarist Paul Chapman joined—temporarily at first—to support and replace Michael Schenker, who would go missing in action.

Drummer Andy Parker maintained that to truly appreciate UFO, it was essential to see and hear the band live. So, in 1979, UFO released their tour de force double live LP *Strangers in the Night*, documenting performances in Chicago and Louisville. It is widely recognized as one of the best live rock recordings of all time. Schenker left again for various reasons.

Michael Schenker.

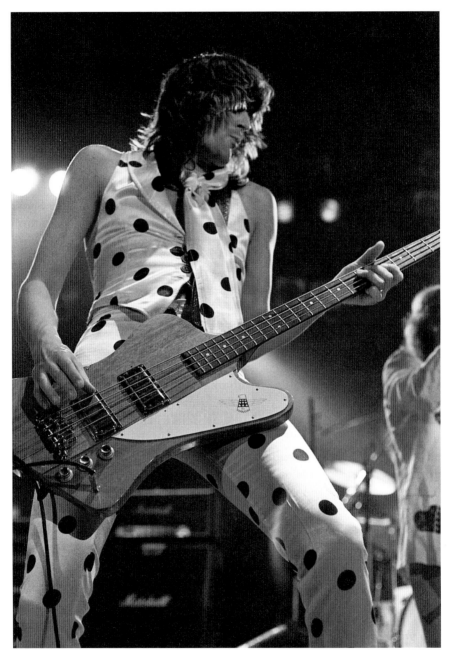

Pete Way.

MICHAEL SCHENKER: I got scared and left. I knew staying with UFO meant more touring and drinking. I've had stage fright all my life and to stand there and enjoy the show, I had to have some drinks. It became very exhausting. I wasn't making any money being in UFO.

As their popularity waned, UFO transitioned. Stability and wisdom replaced unpredictability and irresponsibility. In 1993, the classic lineup of Mogg, Way, Raymond, Parker and Schenker reunited for the 1995 album *Walk on Water*. In the new millennium, lineup configurations included former and new members, including Vinnie Moore on guitar. In late 2022, it took a heart attack to keep Phil Mogg from hitting the stage for a farewell tour. Mogg doesn't ponder the "what ifs?"

There is nothing you can do to change it. I've enjoyed every minute of it.

MUSICAL INFLUENCES WHO MATTER

Pink Floyd, the Jimi Hendrix Experience, Screaming Jay Hawkins, Sonny Boy Williamson, Muddy Waters, Willie Dixon, Howlin' Wolf, Steve Marriott, Arthur Brown, Joe Cocker, Terry Reid, Jeff Beck, the Beatles, the Rolling Stones, Led Zeppelin, Deep Purple, Queen, the Who, Cream, Blue Cheer, Geezer Butler, Wishbone Ash, Mountain, Ian McLagan, Steve Winwood.

PROBABLE CONCERT SETLIST:
INTERNATIONAL AMPHITHEATER, OCTOBER 13, 1978

"Hot 'n' Ready," "Pack It Up (And Go)," "Cherry," "Let It Roll," "Love to Love," "Only You Can Rock Me," "Ain't No Baby," "Out in the Street," "Doctor Doctor," "Lights Out," "Rock Bottom," "Too Hot to Handle," "Shoot Shoot."

YES

FORMED 1968

BAND MEMBERS WHO MATTER

Jon Anderson (lead vocals, other instruments), Chris Squire (bass, vocals), Bill Bruford (drums, percussion), Tony Kaye (keyboards), Steve Howe (guitars, other stringed instruments, vocals), Rick Wakeman (keyboards), Alan White (drums, percussion), Trevor Rabin (guitar, vocals, keyboards).

> CHRIS SQUIRE: Anyone who enjoyed stuff like "Roundabout" wondered why we'd choose to do something so left field. But in retrospect, I think that enabled the band to have as long a career as we've had, because people looked [at] us as risk takers.

WHY THEY MATTER

The joys or derisions of progressive rock are in the mind of the beholder. Whatever your mindset, there has been no finer purveyor of the genre than the band Yes and few more globally successful. Their music was complex but also accessible without clinging to standard rock and pop formulas.

Yes resisted the pressure to produce hit singles yet crafted radio-friendly songs like "Roundabout," "I've Seen All Good People," "Long Distance Runaround," "Yours Is No Disgrace," "Owner of a Lonely Heart" and "It Can Happen."

Chris Squire.

The band was a revolving door for personnel. Approximately twenty different members representing five countries were part of the Yes family.

STEVE HOWE: [Yes] is like a coral reef. This little reef grows up and before it knows, everybody's come and lived in it.

It all began with singer Jon Anderson and bassist Chris Squire. Anderson sang on every Yes album through 2003, the only exception being *Drama* in 1980. The diminutive vocalist had a gift for lyrics drawn from new age spirituality and literature. He possessed a choirboy-like singing voice that could cut through the volume of a rock band without exaggerated enunciation.

Prior to his death in 2015, Chris Squire was the only member to be part of every lineup. His active bass technique and well-pronounced tone was his instrumental calling card.

Anderson and Squire envisioned a band that blended grand vocals with superior instrumentalists. They found the latter in drummer Bill Bruford, guitarist Peter Banks and organist Tony Kaye. The original Yes lineup was born.

ALAN WHITE: It's a challenging band to be in. Everyone [must] be right on it or else the whole thing falls to pieces.

In 1968, Yes caught a break by filling a spot vacated by Sly and the Family Stone. A month later, they opened for Cream at the legendary Farewell Cream concert and earned a coveted residency at London's Marquee Club. A year later, the quintet opened for Janis Joplin. Atlantic Records founder Ahmet Ertegun personally signed them to a record deal.

It took three albums before the band found its signature sound. *The Yes Album* hit the record bins in 1971 with new guitarist Steve Howe replacing Peter Banks. With their fourth album, *Fragile*, keyboardist Rick Wakeman replaced Tony Kaye, and the band's following went from cult to international.

The flamboyant Wakeman gave the band a player who was willing to exploit the sounds of the era's new musical instrument—the Moog synthesizer. His colorful personality and stacks of keyboards were a concert attraction. Roger Dean had also joined the Yes family. As an artist and designer, Dean created the band's all-important visual imagery.

In 1972, Yes delivered one of prog rock's proudest moments with the universally acclaimed studio LP *Close to the Edge*. The live album *Yessongs*

Steve Howe.

followed a year later, and despite its subpar fidelity, the performances raised the bar for future live prog rock albums.

Then came the much-debated double LP *Tales of Topographic Oceans*. Several critics and band members such as Steve Howe and Rick Wakeman called the material "self-indulgent."

Rick Wakeman.

In 1983, a new lineup that included John Anderson, Tony Kaye and Trevor Rabin recorded the band's multiplatinum album *90125*. The album's essential song was "Owner of a Lonely Heart," the band's only no. 1 U.S. hit. The song and album captured the period's synth-dance sound and found a new audience. Once again, the band toured globally to Yes-hungry audiences.

On June 27, 2015, Chris Squire passed away from a rare form of leukemia. The band's emotional first show without Squire opened with a spotlight on his signature Rickenbacker bass placed where Squire normally stood.

In 2017, Yes finally made it into the Rock & Roll Hall of Fame. Jon Anderson always felt it was inevitable. The 1983 hit song "It Can Happen" was prophetic: "It can happen to you. It can happen to me. It can happen to everyone eventually."

MUSICAL INFLUENCES WHO MATTER

Igor Stravinsky, Franz Liszt, Sibelius, Deep Purple, the Beatles, Buddy Holly, the Everly Brothers, Paul McCartney, John Entwistle, Jack Bruce, Jimi Hendrix, the Beach Boys, Simon and Garfunkel, Buddy Rich, Gene Krupa, Weather Report, Chick Corea, Flavio Sala, Chet Atkins, Wes Montgomery, Django Reinhardt, Charlie Christian, Jimmy Webb, Nina Simone, the Fifth Dimension, Vanilla Fudge, the Nice, Family, Frank Zappa, Keith Emerson, Chicago, Bill Haley, Barney Kessel, Les Paul.

PROBABLE CONCERT SETLIST:
INTERNATIONAL AMPHITHEATER, MARCH 6, 1974

"Siberian Khatru," "And You and I," "Close to the Edge," "The Revealing Science of God (Dance of the Dawn)," "The Ancient (Giants Under the Sun)," "Ritual (Nous Sommes Du Soleil)," "Roundabout," "Starship Trooper."

KING CRIMSON

FORMED 1969

BAND MEMBERS WHO MATTER

Robert Fripp (guitar, mellotron), Michael Giles (drums, vocals), Greg Lake (bass, vocals), Ian McDonald (keyboards, mellotron, sax, flute, clarinet), Peter Sinfield (lyricist, light show), John Wetton (vocals, bass, piano), Bill Bruford (drums), Adrian Belew (guitar, vocals), Tony Levin (bass, Chapman stick).

ROBERT FRIPP: Rock is the most malleable music form we have. Within the rock framework, you can play jazz, classical, trance, Urubu drumming and so on. Anything you like.

WHY THEY MATTER

When King Crimson arrived in 1969, the music press scrambled for new terminology. Progressive rock, art rock and avant-garde rock entered the lexicon. But using these terms to describe King Crimson's music only inflamed Robert Fripp.

One thing is for certain: there was no simple way to categorize the music of King Crimson. Over the band's fifty-one-year history, there was a constant flow of personnel changes and hiatuses. Calling them legends is valid even though their audience was a sizeable cult following.

Robert Fripp.

Throughout King Crimson's entire history, the one constant was co-founder and guiding light, guitarist Robert Fripp. Despite the band's chameleon-like nature, Fripp chose to reuse the King Crimson name for identification and promotional purposes.

ROBERT FRIPP: King Crimson lives in different bodies at different times, and [so] the particular form in which the group takes [will] change.

Crimson grew from the remnants of a 1968 English pop band called Giles, Giles and Fripp. After dissolving, King Crimson emerged when co-founders Robert Fripp and Michael Giles added bassist and tenor, Greg Lake, lyricist Peter Sinfield and multi-instrumentalist Ian McDonald.

The band developed its sound over the next several months, culminating in a free concert in London's Hyde Park. They opened for the Rolling Stones in front of a half-million people. Based on their performance, several record companies came calling.

In late 1969, Crimson released their epochal debut album, *In the Court of the Crimson King*, complete with neo-gothic artwork that made the album cover one of rock's most haunting and recognizable. It jump-started that British prog rock movement and featured screaming guitars, saxophones, woodwinds and other acoustic instruments supported by the Mellotron keyboard. Their music was challenging but rewarding for the open-minded.

The LP's most memorable track is "21st Century Schizoid Man." In 1995, Fripp told *Rolling Stone*'s Sylvie Simmons that it represented his interpretation of Jimi Hendrix playing Stravinsky's "Rite of Spring." Pete Townshend of the Who called the album an "uncanny masterpiece." But the LP marked the end of the original lineup. It wasn't until ten years later that a King Crimson lineup lasted for more than one studio album.

Around 1972, a new lineup embraced a heavier and more progressive fusion sound. The result was *Lark's Tongues in Aspic*, a studio work that rivaled Crimson's magnificent debut. *Rolling Stone* magazine called Crimson's sound "brainy gothic metal." Again, the lineup was short-lived and included Fripp (guitar, mellotron), John Wetton (bass), David Cross (violin), Jamie Muir (percussion) and Bill Bruford (drums).

In 1974, the initial era of Crimson concluded with the critically acclaimed LP *Red*. From inception through 1974, the band's output included six studio and two live albums.

About this time, Fripp's view of the music business had soured. The erudite native of Dorset, England, believed the music industry was grossly

John Wetton.

inefficient. In other words, it made little sense for bands to employ large numbers of people for a few musicians to make music. Fripp believed in the principle of smaller, smarter and more mobile. He rejected the idea that rock musicians had to check their intelligence at the door.

> **BILL BRUFORD:** Robert was the man who coined the term "dinosaur" in reference to these megalithic 1970s rock acts. He did it before Johnny Rotten [Sex Pistols] ever did. Robert presaged punk.

Fripp rarely cared what others thought about his material. He deconstructed and reformed bands with musicians whose abilities and mindset enabled them to join him on his musical journey.

GREG LAKE: We didn't really have a formula. All we knew was the music had a life of its own.

After Crimson's 1974 breakup, Fripp reformed and disbanded the band in various configurations.

Crimson last performed as a band in late 2021. Fripp cryptically tweeted, "A significant moment in time as King Crimson 'moved from sound to silence' today in Japan." Whatever that means, long live the king.

MUSICAL INFLUENCES WHO MATTER

The Beatles, Jimi Hendrix, Bartok, Debussy, Stravinsky, Django Reinhardt, Scotty Moore, Chuck Berry, Eddie Lang, Bernard Stanley Bilk, Tool, Brian Eno.

PROBABLE CONCERT SETLIST:
AUDITORIUM THEATRE, APRIL 25, 1974

"Larks' Tongues in Aspic, Part Two," "Lament," "The Night Watch," "Trio," "Exiles," "Easy Money," "Starless and Bible Black," "Fracture," "21st Century Schizoid Man."

EMERSON, LAKE & PALMER

FORMED 1970

BAND MEMBERS WHO MATTER

Keith Emerson (piano, organ, synthesizer, composer), Greg Lake (bass, guitar, songwriter, vocals, producer), Carl Palmer (drums, percussion).

> FROM THE SONG "KARN EVIL 9": Welcome back my friends to the show that never ends. We're so glad you could attend come inside, come inside. You gotta see the show. It's a dynamo. It's rock and roll...

WHY THEY MATTER

The song "Karn Evil 9" is a tale about the future, but it also said something about the band that wrote it. Along with Led Zeppelin, Emerson, Lake & Palmer (ELP) was among the highest-grossing bands in the mid-1970s. They were a bona fide supergroup—a power trio that emphasized keyboards and percussion.

Unlike prior rock collaborations, the British trio experimented with the classics, jazz, rock, electronica and pop-like ballads. They raised the bar with the sophisticated nature of their material delivered with extraordinary musicianship and stage flamboyance. But these assets eventually led to their unraveling.

Some musicologists suggest that bands like ELP paved the way for the punk rock backlash. But Greg Lake shot back.

GREG LAKE: ELP was music....Punk was fashion. [Punk] had no musical or cultural foundation. It was a creation of the media looking for more cash. If you want to talk about punk, talk about the Who. That's a real punk band. The Sex Pistols were a joke.

ELP's contributions to the world of rock music were unique. They introduced a generation of rockers to composers like Modest Mussorgsky, Alberto Ginastera and Aaron Copeland.

KEITH EMERSON: It's gratifying when schoolteachers introduce classical music to a young class and play ELP versions first, and then analyze them against the original classical pieces.

Another ELP contribution was their use of technology then in its infancy. Along with his grand piano and Hammond organs, Emerson was a pioneering user of the Moog synthesizer. His Frankenstein-like "Monster Moog" weighed in at five hundred pounds and stood ten feet tall. Some of the modules were simply for show.

Drummer Carl Palmer was also a showman who embraced the day's technological possibilities. In 1973, he commissioned British Steel to design and customize a stainless-steel drum kit that augmented his dazzling array of percussion instruments mounted on a rotating platform. It was a beast, but he knew how to get the most out of it.

But it was Greg Lake's acoustic ballads, meticulous production skills and wide vocal range that gave ELP wider appeal. Songs like "Lucky Man," "C'est La Vie," "Take a Pebble," "In the Beginning" and "Still...You Turn Me On," were ideal for radio airplay.

ELP began when in 1969, Emerson and Lake struck up a friendship when their respective bands—the Nice and King Crimson—shared a gig. The two envisioned a future in music together. They talked about bringing in drummer Mitch Mitchell of the Jimi Hendrix Experience, but music impresario Robert Stigwood suggested Carl Palmer—a nineteen-year-old who played in cult bands. An audition produced an immediate chemistry.

Between 1970 and 1975, ELP released six LPs, including a three-record live recording that captured their legendary stage shows. All climbed high

Keith Emerson (*left*) and Greg Lake.

Greg Lake.

up the charts (particularly in the United Kingdom) and earned gold sales certification.

By 1977, tensions were growing. The band released a double album titled *Works Volume 1*. Three sides served as solo vehicles while a fourth featured collaborative work. A tour was mounted, but Emerson's contribution needed heavy orchestration, and the result was financially draining.

Following a less than stellar seventh studio album, the band collapsed under the weight of costly and physically draining tours and diverging musical interests. In the years that followed, ELP reunited in part or in full, including a one-off fortieth anniversary show (2010) in London.

Over the years, Emerson and Lake expressed disappointment with the state of the music industry, but Carl Palmer advised: "Just remember to look at all forms of music because the more music you understand the more you [can] correspond with other musicians, and the more knowledge you will have. You can't believe what's written about you. Be your own judge."

In 2016, both Greg Lake and Keith Emerson died. The show that never ends did…or did it? In 2022, Carl Palmer reunited with his deceased bandmates through the wonders of technology. His world tour was named Welcome Back My Friends—The Return of Emerson Lake in Palmer.

MUSICAL INFLUENCES WHO MATTER

Fats Waller, Oscar Peterson, Dave Brubeck, Jack McDuff, Big John Patton, J.S. Bach, Aaron Copland, Dmitri Shostakovich, Bela Bartok, Winifred Atwell, Alberto Ginastera, Elvis Presley, Little Richard, Sergei Prokofiev, Gene Krupa, Buddy Rich, Elvin Jones, Joe Morello, Philly Joe Jones.

PROBABLE CONCERT SETLIST:
INTERNATIONAL AMPHITHEATER, DECEMBER 2, 1973

"Hoedown," "Jerusalem," "Toccata," "Tarkus," "Benny the Bouncer," "Take a Pebble," "Lucky Man," "Piano Improvisation," "Take a Pebble," "The Endless Enigma," "Karn Evil 9," "Pictures at an Exhibition," "Blue Rondo a la Turk."

GENESIS

FORMED 1967

BAND MEMBERS WHO MATTER

Mike Rutherford (bass, guitar, vocals), Peter Gabriel (lead vocals, flute, percussion), Tony Banks (keyboards, vocals), Steve Hackett (guitar), Phil Collins (drums, lead vocals).

> **MIKE RUTHERFORD:** We went from being a cult band, to a big cult band, to a band with mass appeal.

WHY THEY MATTER

Known for their complex song structures, elaborate instrumentation and theatrical performances, the seeds of Genesis took root when schoolmates Peter Gabriel, Tony Banks, Mike Rutherford and Anthony Phillips joined a part-time songwriting collective. Although their parents pushed for a university education, music proved too enticing.

The band's first two albums and singles flopped commercially. They shuffled through drummers and lost co-founding guitarist/composer Anthony Phillips to fragile health and stage fright. Two positions needed filling.

Phil Collins responded to a want ad. He had played in various London bands while studying drama and acting. Meanwhile, guitarist Steve Hackett was looking for a gig. The chemistry was good, and three became five.

Peter Gabriel.

Although co-founders Tony Banks and Mike Rutherford played on every Genesis album, fans and music chroniclers view Genesis as having two periods: the Peter Gabriel era from 1967 to 1975 and the Phil Collins era from 1975 to 1996.

With the classic lineup in place, the quintet found their musical footing with their third studio album—*Nursery Cryme*. They went from a cult band to a big cult band over the next three albums. The culmination was *The Lamb Lies Down on Broadway*, a conceptual double LP that tells the surreal story of young Puerto Rican living in New York City. It was the Gabriel era's most ambitious project.

185

Peter Gabriel.

Throughout this period, Gabriel took his rock theatrics to a new level with ornate costumes, makeup and hair styles.

> **TONY BANKS:** His costumes during live performances often made it impossible for him to get a microphone anywhere near his mouth!

The Lamb's supporting tour was an arduous and costly one. Gabriel's artistic priorities were shifting. Tensions were growing. In 1975, Peter Gabriel and Genesis parted ways, and Gabriel went on to an enormously successful solo career.

Having lost their frontman and identity, Genesis auditioned many vocalists and then realized his replacement was already in the band. Drummer Phil Collins had already provided vocal support and, as an insider, was likely to be accepted as Gabriel's replacement.

Their first post-Gabriel album, *Trick of the Tail*, sold more than all prior Genesis albums. But as the band prepared for their next studio effort, Hackett was eyeing his departure. The guitarist felt like an outsider and discovered the rewards of working solo.

The band was now a trio and went from a big cult band to a mass appeal band. Their 1978 album was appropriately titled *And Then There Were Three*. From this point forward, Genesis attracted a massive new audience and experienced a long period of unimaginable success with a series of top-selling albums and hit songs.

Coinciding with this period, Phil Collins was building an equally successful solo career with power-pop hits. Banks and Rutherford also pursued solo projects, but like moths to a flame, Genesis was home. Meanwhile, original fans blamed Collins for turning their beloved art rock cult band into a commercial pop music machine.

> **PHIL COLLINS:** I became a target for no apparent reason. I only make the records once and it's the radio [stations] that play them all the time. I mean, [me] the Antichrist?

In 1997, Phil Collins quit, citing family issues and other projects. Banks and Rutherford recorded the band's last studio album with a new vocalist. Then came the difficult decision to end Genesis.

Fans were ecstatic when Collins, Banks and Rutherford reunited for a tour in 2007. It was the second-highest-grossing tour of the year and the most elaborate and expensive the band had undertaken. Meanwhile, Phil Collins's health issues were making drumming increasingly more difficult.

Fifty-three years following their first live gig, the band gave its final performance with Phil Collins seated onstage. London's O2 arena was the final stop on their Last Domino tour. Peter Gabriel was in the audience. During the show, Phil Collins quipped, "After tonight, we've all got to get real jobs."

MUSICAL INFLUENCES WHO MATTER

The Rolling Stones, Peter Green (Fleetwood Mac), Paul Butterfield, the Beatles, King Crimson, the Kinks, the Jimi Hendrix Experience, Yes, Gentle Giant, Moody Blues, Bee Gees, Simon and Garfunkel, Alan Price (The Animals), Buddy Rich, the Mahavishnu Orchestra, Weather Report, Nina Simone, Otis Redding.

PROBABLE CONCERT SETLIST:
AUDITORIUM THEATRE, APRIL 11, 1974

"Watcher of the Skies," "Dancing with the Moonlit Knight," "The Cinema Show," "I Know What I Like (In Your Wardrobe)," "Firth of Fifth," "The Musical Box," "Horizons," "The Battle of Epping Forest," "Supper's Ready," "The Knife."

MAHAVISHNU ORCHESTRA

FORMED 1971

BAND MEMBERS WHO MATTER

John McLaughlin (lead guitar), Jerry Goodman (violin, guitar), Jan Hammer (keyboards), Rick Laird (bass), Billy Cobham (drums, percussion), John Luc Ponty (violin), Gayle Moran (keyboards), Ralphe Armstrong (bass), Narada Michael Walden (drums, percussion).

> JOHN McLAUGHLIN: It was about connecting music to the spiritual, the universal, the stuff beyond. So, when people asked: "Is it jazz? Is it rock?" I would laugh and say, "I don't know. What do you think?"

WHY THEY MATTER

In the early to mid-1960s, a young guitarist from Yorkshire, England, gigged in an array of British bands along with session work. Then, John McLaughlin's life changed when he listened to *A Love Supreme* by jazz great John Coltrane. Spirituality became the center of his search for existence and meaning.

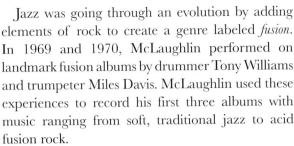

Jazz was going through an evolution by adding elements of rock to create a genre labeled *fusion*. In 1969 and 1970, McLaughlin performed on landmark fusion albums by drummer Tony Williams and trumpeter Miles Davis. McLaughlin used these experiences to record his first three albums with music ranging from soft, traditional jazz to acid fusion rock.

On his fourth album—*My Goals Beyond*—the guitarist explored Indian and acoustic music with the help of violinist Jerry Goodman (former Flock) and drummer extraordinaire Billy Cobham. Both would follow McLaughlin on a musical adventure unlike any previously experienced.

That adventure was the Mahavishnu Orchestra, one of the most genre-bending groups ever assembled and the gold standard for high-energy jazz-rock fusion. It was Indian spiritual leader Sri Chinmoy who inspired McLaughlin (along with Carlos Santana) and gave him the name Mahavishnu.

The Orchestra's original lineup was a model of diversity and abilities: Chicagoan Jerry Goodman was a classically trained violinist and American Jew whose mother played with the Chicago Symphony Orchestra, Billy Cobham was a Panamanian-born African American drummer, bassist Rick Laird was a native of Ireland and keyboardist Jan Hammer was a native of Czechoslovakia.

McLaughlin surrounded himself with musicians who could not only keep up with his speed, technique and improvisation but whose limits he could push as well.

John McLaughlin.

RICK LAIRD: Most of our music is just a skeleton structure. That must be with time signatures like 9/8 and 10/8. We're all going in the same direction but trying not to plan too far in advance. Anyone can pull out which changes the whole course of the composition. That's when you hear real music because you can't rely on past experiences.

JERRY GOODMAN: When it came time to solo, I was a bit in the weeds. I had the technique, but I never played anything [in those odd time signatures]. It was all new to me, so I just kept thinking... help...get me through this please! It was trial by fire learning this incredibly difficult music. Trading solos with John was something inspiring and brought me to a new level.

BILLY COBHAM: [Rick Laird] was the most dependable person in the band. He played what was necessary to keep the rest of us from going off our musical rails.

Between 1971 and 1973, the original Mahavishnu Orchestra released two studio albums and a live recording. The original band's last official studio album *Birds of Fire* cracked the Billboard Top 20 rock charts—an unheard-of accomplishment for a jazz-rock album. Additional tracks completed prior to the original band's breakup were released in 1999 as *The Lost Trident Sessions*.

The band's biographer, Walter Kolosky, pinpointed the band's duality with delicate and graceful songs like "A Lotus on Irish Streams": "How could this be the same band that just blew out my eardrums?"

McLaughlin reformed the Mahavishnu Orchestra between 1974 and 1976 with new members and released three albums during that period: *Apocalypse, Visions of the Emerald Beyond* and *Inner Worlds*. New members included Jean-Luc Ponty on violin, Gayle Moran on keyboards, Ralphe Armstrong on bass and Narada Michael Walden on drums. From 1984 through 1986, he reformed Mahavishnu again, but no lineup had the incendiary impact of the original.

JOHN MCLAUGHLIN'S MUSICAL INFLUENCES WHO MATTER

John Coltrane, Cannonball Adderley, Bill Evans, Django Reinhardt, Stephane Grappelli, Thelonius Monk, Charles Mingus, Sonny Rollins, Miles Davis, Herbie Hancock, Oscar Peterson, Pat Metheny, the Eagles, the Beatles, Jimi Hendrix, Eric Clapton, Sly and the Family Stone, Bela Bartok, Igor Stravinsky, Maurice Ravel, Claude Debussy, Anton Webern, Buddy Guy, Muddy Waters, B.B. King, Big Bill Broonzy, Sonny Terry, Leadbelly and a long list of Indian musicians.

PROBABLE CONCERT SETLIST: ARIE CROWN THEATER, MAY 8, 1975

"Eternity's Breath Pt. I," "Eternity's Breath Pt. II," "Lila's Dance."

FRANK ZAPPA

GUITAR, SYNCLAVIER, BANDLEADER, SONGWRITER, COMPOSER, ARRANGER, FREE SPEECH ADVOCATE

FRANK ZAPPA: I like to carry things to their most ridiculous extreme because out there on the fringe is where my type of entertainment lies.

WHY HE MATTERS

Frank Vincent Zappa was among rock 'n' roll's sharpest musical minds and most astute social satirists. Everything was fair game for the mustachioed master of musical idioms. He was a respected musician, composer, filmmaker, producer and innovator and the only artist to be inducted into both the Rock & Roll and Jazz Halls of Fame.

The Rock & Roll Hall of Fame called him "the most prolific composer of his generation who bridged rock, jazz, classical, doo-wop, avant-garde, and novelty forms with masterful ease."

Weirdness was Zappa's trademark. His lyrics and song titles were designed to provoke: "Sexually Aroused Gas Mask," "Stink-Foot," "Smell My Beard" and "Nanook Rubs It" just to name a few. Even his playful sense of humor extended to his children's names: Moon Unit, Dweezil, Diva Muffin and Ahmet Emuukha Rodan.

When interviewed, Zappa was forthright and insightful when challenged intelligently. When confronted with stupidity, he could be abrupt and snippy. Although he looked like a counter-culture hippie, he was far from one. He avoided recreational drugs and alcohol and was a devoted father and spouse.

When he was a child, his family was on the move as a result of his father's defense industry job. During his high school years, Zappa and schoolmate Don Van Vliet (better known as Captain Beefheart) listened to records well into the night and often missed school.

Unlike most people his age, Zappa was taken by the complex sounds of modern-era composers like Edgard Varèse, Igor Stravinsky and Anton Webern. By his early twenties, he was involved in an array of music and film industry ventures and other life experiences. But the boundaries-pushing musician needed a vehicle for his ideas. He joined an Orange County (California) band named the Soul Giants and persuaded members to play his music. The Soul Giants became The Mothers. When Verve/MGM insisted on a less controversial name, they became The Mothers of Invention.

> **FRANK ZAPPA:** We starved for ten months because the type of music we played was grossly unpopular in that area. Audiences couldn't identify with it, so we got into the habit of insulting the audience and we made a big reputation that way. Nobody came to hear us play.... They came to see how much abuse they could take, and they loved it.

The band's 1966 debut album *Freak-Out* skewered American culture. Paul McCartney cited it as a blueprint for the Beatles' 1967 *Sgt. Pepper's* album. The Mothers incorporated woodwinds, brass, bizarre harmonics, electronically altered sounds—and unusual time signatures and percussion techniques.

When the original lineup disbanded three years later, Zappa launched a solo career with the album *Hot Rats*, an all-instrumental showcase for his guitar playing.

Zappa broke through commercially with the 1974 album *Apostrophe (')* and his first charting single, "Don't Eat the Yellow Snow." In 1979, he scored another hit with the disco dancing send-up "Dancin' Fool."

During the 1980s, Zappa recorded several orchestral compositions with the London Symphony Orchestra while scoring another hit with the 1982 novelty single "Valley Girl." It featured daughter Moon Unit delivering a monologue of laughable slang phrases used by teenage girls in the San Fernando Valley.

In 1984, Zappa discovered the Synclavier, an early digital keyboard and workstation. It enabled him to make his 1986 Grammy-winning album, *Jazz from Hell.*

Frank Zappa.

A year later, Zappa (along with Dee Snyder and others) famously made headlines by appearing before a Senate subcommittee on offensive music lyrics. Zappa surprised the committee and viewers with his conservative appearance and articulate testimony.

Zappa embarked on his final North American and European tour in 1988. Three years later, it was revealed that he had inoperable prostate cancer. In one of his last interviews, Zappa talked with Jamie Gangel of the *Today Show*. Gangel revealed, "He was still funny, opinionated and off-the-wall. But you could tell it was very tough for him to get through that interview."

But even terminal cancer couldn't stifle Zappa's wit. When asked how he'd like to be remembered, he responded, "It's not important to even be remembered. People who want to be remembered are guys like Reagan and Bush who spend lots of money and work to make sure they will be remembered terrifically." Frank Vincent Zappa died on December 4, 1993.

MUSICAL INFLUENCES WHO MATTER

Edgard Varèse, Igor Stravinsky, Béla Bartók, Anton Webern, Arnold Schoenberg, the Penguins, Little Anthony, Spike Jones, Johnny Otis, Jimi Hendrix, Cream, the Rolling Stones, Bob Dylan, Traffic, Wes Montgomery, Johnny "Guitar" Watson, Howlin' Wolf, Muddy Waters, Hubert Sumlin, Guitar Slim, John Coltrane, Clarence "Gatemouth" Brown, Allan Holdsworth, Jeff Beck, Eric Clapton, Walter Gerwig, Warren DeMartini, Jake E. Lee.

PROBABLE CONCERT SETLIST:
NORTHERN ILLINOIS UNIVERSITY, APRIL 27, 1974

"Pygmy Twylyte," "Dummy Up," "The Idiot Bastard Son," "Cheepnis," "Inca Roads," "Cosmik Debris," "Montana," "Improvisation," "Dupree's Paradise," "It Can't Happen Here," "Hungry Freaks, Daddy," "You're Probably Wondering Why I'm Here," "How Could I Be Such a Fool?," "I Ain't Got No Heart," "I'm Not Satisfied," "Wowie Zowie," "Let's Make the Water Turn Black," "Harry, You're a Beast," "The Orange County Lumber Truck," "Oh No," "Son of Orange County," "Trouble Every Day," "Penguin in Bondage," "Andy," "Camarillo Brillo."

ROBIN TROWER

ELECTRIC GUITAR, BANDLEADER, SONGWRITER

ROBIN TROWER: To be spoken in the same breath or sentence as Hendrix was a great thing you know! At the same time, I felt people were missing what I was doing because they couldn't see beyond it.

WHY HE MATTERS

In an era where guitar heroes are out of fashion, Robin reminds us how the electric guitar reshaped popular music and launched careers. The Catford, England native burst onto the scene when he was needed most. The 1970 death of Jimi Hendrix left a void, and Trower filled it. Far from an imitator, Robin mixed soul, funk, blues and rock to create music all his own.

As a teenager, Robin turned to his older brother's record collection for early influences, but it was the modern tone and phrasing of Jimi Hendrix that punctuated his playing.

The pug-nosed guitarist began his career in 1964 with the rhythm 'n' blues outfit the Paramounts. A few years later, they were far better known as Procol Harum. Between 1967 and 1971, he capably filled a supporting role until several guitar-driven songs appeared on the albums *Home* and *Broken Barricades*. To borrow a phrase from the wife of Willy Loman in Arthur Miller's play *Death of a Salesman*, attention must be paid.

Robin Trower.

A transformative moment arrived when Trower discovered the voicing of the Fender Stratocaster guitar. During a Procol Harum tour with Jethro Tull, Trower noodled with Martin Barre's guitar and had an "ah-ha" moment.

With Trower and his band headed in different directions, he left to form the short-lived quartet Jude. For his next project, he recruited former Procol Harum bandmate Matthew Fischer (for his production expertise) and Beatles engineer Geoff Emerick. Trower added former Stone the Crows bassist James Dewar and Aruban-born drummer Reg Isidore to complete the Robin Trower power trio.

The trio's 1973 debut album *Twice Removed from Yesterday* was a work in progress, with Trower's playing drawing comparisons to the late Jimi Hendrix. There were commonalities between the two in terms of technique, gear and tone, but the emotion and musical exploration were distinctly Trower's. Bassist James Dewar's deep, soulful voice gave the music a sense of mystery and otherworldliness. Drummer Reg Isidore added the propulsion.

Then came the band's 1974 critically acclaimed album *Bridge of Sighs*. It reinforced Trower's reputation as a "guitar god." The album jumped to no. 7 and resided thirty-one weeks on the U.S. charts. Comparisons to Hendrix grew.

In a 1998 interview, Trower explained that he was trying to make a rhythm 'n' blues album that combined James Brown, B.B. King and Donny Hathaway with the rock of Jimi Hendrix and Cream.

Following *Bridge of Sighs*, Reg Isidore was replaced by ex–Sly Stone drummer Bill Lordan, who played with Trower through 1981. During this period, the trio filled arenas and stadiums. Lordan was a funky, hard-hitting drummer, who tightened up the music.

> **BILL LORDAN:** When we did *For Earth Below*, I had only been with the band two or three months. I'd just left Sly [Stone] and we didn't have time to get tight. Now that we've played together for a year, we've got it down to a science.

James Dewar remained by Robin's side until 1983. He died in 2002 from a rare medical condition. Reg Isidore passed away in 2009.

> **ROBIN TROWER:** Jimmy was very gifted and had a wonderful voice. We had a fantastic relationship, and we were like brothers. He was a very sweet guy.

Through the mid-1980s, Robin made ten albums for Chrysalis Records. Eight consecutive LPs broke the Top 40 on Billboard's Top 200. But Trower grew weary of nonstop touring and headlining huge venues. Disillusionment with the music industry (a common theme) was another matter.

Trower worked on his songwriting skills and spent more time with family. He made albums with ex-Cream bassist Jack Bruce and one with original

Left to right: James Dewar, Robin Trower and Bill Lordan.

drummer Reg Isidore. During a self-imposed exile, Trower regained his inspiration and perspective. His desire to perform returned.

The 2000s sparked a new era of Trower pride. He focused more on songcraft than guitar parts although there was still plenty of that to satisfy fans. He recorded material based on his standards rather than standards imposed by the music industry. Fans still flock to see the guitar great perform live.

> ROBIN TROWER: I love the guitar as much now as when I began....I think I'm a bit more musical as a guitarist now. I'm better technically, but it's not like I'm faster—just more fluid. I'm still trying to do the same thing I always have—hit that note that stings you in the heart.

MUSICAL INFLUENCES WHO MATTER

Scotty Moore, Otis Rush, Hubert Sumlin, B.B. King, Albert King, James Brown, Howlin' Wolf, T-Bone Walker, Buddy Guy, Lowell Fulson, Son House, John Lee Hooker, Jimi Hendrix, Jimmie Vaughan, Billy Gibbons, Steve Cropper, Curtis Mayfield, Elvis Presley, Gene Vincent.

PROBABLE CONCERT SETLIST:
AUDITORIUM THEATRE, MARCH 28, 1975

"Day of the Eagle," "Bridge of Sighs," "Gonna Be More Suspicious," "Lady Love," "Daydream," "Too Rolling Stoned," "I Can't Wait Much Longer," "Alethea," "Little Bit of Sympathy," "The Fool and Me," "Rock Me Baby."

WISHBONE ASH

FORMED 1969

BAND MEMBERS WHO MATTER

Andy Powell (guitar, vocals), Steve Upton (drums), Martin Turner (bass, vocals), Ted Turner (guitar, vocals), Laurie Wisefield (guitar, banjo, vocals), Bob Skeat (bass, backing vocals).

> **ANDY POWELL:** We wanted to do something with guitars that hadn't been already thrashed to death. [Guitar soloing] had become such a bore. We wanted to evolve our own sound.

WHY THEY MATTER

Over fifty-two years ago, Wishbone Ash was named best new band by the British publications *Melody Maker* and *Sounds*. A year later, readers of *New Music Express* and *Sounds* voted *Argus* "Album of the Year." By the end of 1974, they had toured the United States an exhausting seventeen times.

Wishbone Ash built their following one album and venue at a time without gimmicks or Top 40 songs. The band persevered through numerous changes in personnel, record labels, music trends and legal entanglements. And fifty-two years later, Ash continues to power through with the passion and torch-bearing responsibility of original member Andy Powell.

Andy Powell.

Ash's brand of progressive music knitted together English folk rock, blues, boogie and bits of jazz. Their lyrics drew from mythology, fantasy and even the Bible.

During the 1970s, the quartet shared the stage with some of rock's biggest acts. Their calling card was—and still is—the melodic and sophisticated interaction between their two lead guitarists (Andy Powell has been there throughout). Bands like Thin Lizzy, Aerosmith, Iron Maiden, Lynyrd Skynyrd and even the Eagles have acknowledged the Ash influence.

The origins of Wishbone Ash harken back to 1966 when bassist Martin Turner, his guitarist-brother Glen Turner and drummer Steve Upton played together semiprofessionally. When guitarist Glen Turner quit, Martin and Steve Upton placed a want ad for a lead guitarist. Andy Powell and Ted Turner (no relation to bassist Martin Turner) responded. Choosing just one proved too difficult, so both were selected. The idea of hiring a guitarist and a keyboard player was scrapped.

> ANDY POWELL: We decided to really use the guitars as a horn section. One of the first songs we ever wrote was "Blind Eye," and that song really used guitars just like horns in those horn bands.

In late 1969, the band opened for Deep Purple. During a sound check, Andy Powell and Ritchie Blackmore traded licks, and Blackmore offered to help Ash get a record deal.

A year later, Ash released a strong, self-titled debut album. The dual-lead guitars of Powell and Ted Turner were a powerful component in the compositional mix of English folk, prog, blues and boogie. And rather than feature a dominant lead vocalist, the band relied on shared vocal harmonies.

After a heavy touring schedule, they offered a mix of styles on their 1971 studio release *Pilgrimage*. A year later, Ash released their most imaginative and essential studio album. With its medieval themes, *Argus* climbed to no. 3 in the United Kingdom and turned the band into arena headliners.

Riding the success of *Argus*, *Wishbone Four* climbed even higher up the U.S. Billboard 200. It was their first self-produced studio album and their most mature and successful to date. That same year, the band captured their exciting live performances on vinyl. The album *Live Dates* was a hallmark of 1970s live albums.

The first of many changes took place in 1974. Ted Turner departed and left the band's future uncertain. The technically proficient Laurie Wisefield took his spot—but there was an adjustment period.

Ups and downs followed. The album *Locked In* was a step backward. The band parted ways with longtime manager Miles Copeland III and relocated to America. A female vocalist was employed to expand the band's commercial reach.

Through it all, Ash retained a respectable degree of popularity. The final appearance of the Powell-Turner-Upton-Wisefield lineup occurred in late 1980. Original members reunited for the 1987 all-instrumental album *Nouveau Calls* and toured together for the first time in fourteen years.

An elevated degree of legal acrimony between Powell and original members followed. The courts eventually ruled in Andy Powell's favor regarding the Wishbone Ash name. How long does Powell intend to keep the band's legacy alive?

ANDY POWELL: The band has been my sustenance. To me, it's the gift that keeps on giving. It's a beacon of positivity in my life and in however great and small way, in the lives of others. And I'll keep the beast alive as long as I can...as long as it feels right.

MUSICAL INFLUENCES WHO MATTER

Hank Marvin, Johnny Kidd, Django Reinhardt, Chuck Berry, the Everly Brothers, Little Richard, Wayne Fontana, Ray Charles, Elvis Presley, Pete Townshend, Peter Green, Fleetwood Mac, B.B. King, Eric Clapton, Cream, the Beatles, the Rolling Stones, the Animals, Pentangle, Steve Cropper, Fairport Convention, Albert Lee, John Mayall, Sam and Dave, Otis Redding, Marvin Gaye, James Brown, Steve Miller, the Doobie Brothers.

PROBABLE CONCERT SETLIST:
AUDITORIUM THEATRE, AUGUST 13, 1973

"The King Will Come," "Warrior," "Throw Down the Sword," "The Pilgrim," Rock 'n' Roll Widow," "Jail Bait," "Ballad of the Beacon," "Baby What You Want Me to Do," "Lady Whiskey," "Phoenix," "Blowin' Free."

Opposite: Martin Turner (*left*) and Ted Turner.

Ian Hunter.

MOTT THE HOOPLE

FORMED 1969

BAND MEMBERS WHO MATTER

Dale "Buffin" Griffin (drums), Peter Overend Watts (bass), Verden Allen (organ), Mick Ralphs (guitar), Ian Hunter (lead vocals, piano, guitar), Luther Grosvenor, aka Ariel Bender (guitar), Morgan Fisher (keyboards).

> **BRIAN MAY:** Mott would swing relentlessly and unstoppably into their show every night, like a marauding band of outlaws. And every night there was something close to a riot—the kids couldn't get close enough to the stage—they simply couldn't get enough.

WHY THEY MATTER

In Shakespeare's *Romeo and Juliet*, Juliet asks "What's in a name?" A lot in the case of Mott the Hoople. British music industry figure Guy Stevens named the band after character Norman Mott, a lazy scammer in the 1966 underground comic novel *Mott the Hoople*. Stevens thought the name would look cool on a venue marquee.

As for the band, they left a footprint disproportionately greater than their five years of music making and record sales. The band was a cast of characters. When Queen toured with Mott the Hoople in 1974, Brian May described them as "an agglomeration of bright colors, bizarre shapes, scarves, leather, sunglasses, velvet, huge boots and strange felt hats all blending seamlessly into the masses of hair, beer bottles and battered guitar cases covered with stickers."

In every way, members lived the rock 'n' roll lifestyle and connected with working-class kids. They had a profound influence on bands like Queen, David Bowie, Kiss, the Clash, Motley Crew and Def Leppard.

It all started with Guy Stevens—a lovable and loony British music impresario. He envisioned a band that married the sounds of an electric Bob Dylan, the Rolling Stones, Procol Harum and Jerry Lee Lewis. Seems crazy. He auditioned musicians Verden Allen, Dale Griffin, Mick Ralphs, Overland Watts and Stan Tippins of the band Silence.

All but singer Tippins fit Steven's vision of an image-conscious frontman. Filling that role was Ian Hunter—a sunglasses-wearing singer who had a Dylan-like delivery, piano playing ability and lots of curly hair. Stevens renamed the group Mott the Hoople and secured a recording contract with newly formed Island Records.

IAN HUNTER: For Guy [Stevens] to see anything in me was quite incredible because there was nothing there to see. I mean, there was something there, but it was [buried] about three layers [deep] which he saw but which nobody else had ever seen.

Mott made four albums in the next three years. Although mass media failed to "get them," a new breed of young fans was attending their concerts. But record sales failed to meet expectations. Their record company had given up on them. They were playing to thinning audiences and experienced a few Spinal Tap–worthy moments. Morale was low.

Voila…David Bowie stepped in. As a Mott fan, he offered his song "Suffragette City." It was rejected and became a hit for Bowie. He then offered the song "All the Young Dudes." Ian Hunter's ears heard smash hit when Bowie played it on acoustic guitar. So did Dale Griffin: "I'm thinking, 'He wants to give us that? He must be crazy!'"

The band fleshed out the song, and Bowie helped them sign with CBS/ Columbia. In mid-1972, "All the Young Dudes" was released as a single, and the song hit pay dirt. The album of the same name (with Bowie producing and arranging) achieved chart success. The audiences returned and financial fortunes changed.

But success was a double-edged sword. The glam aspect of the new Mott ran counter to their earlier image. Old fans felt abandoned. New

Ian Hunter.

fans hoped David Bowie would appear at shows. Although welcoming the success, band members Verden Allen and Mick Ralphs were not happy with the band's new image and with management urging Hunter to take more control.

With a rejuvenated Mott the Hoople, Ian Hunter responded by writing some of his best material for the 1973 album *Mott*. It was the band's highest charting on both sides of the pond. The singles "Honaloochie Boogie" and "All the Way from Memphis" rose to no. 12 and no. 10 respectively on the U.K. charts.

With Allen and Ralphs replaced by Morgan Fisher (keyboards) and Ariel Bender (guitar), Mott recorded *The Hoople* in 1974, their final album of original material. It was well received, but the band had nearly reached its end. The band's history becomes muddled after Bowie guitarist Mick Ronson joined and Ian Hunter departed.

MUSICAL INFLUENCES WHO MATTER

Tommy Steele, Hank Marvin, Chuck Berry, Little Richard, Liberace, the Rolling Stones, Steve Cropper, Booker T. Jones, the Beatles, Moby Grape, Eddie Cochran, James Burton, Buddy Holly, Buffalo Springfield, Leslie West, Jimmy Smith, Jimmy McGriff, Richard Holmes, Ted Heath, Count Basie.

PROBABLE CONCERT SETLIST:
AUDITORIUM THEATRE, OCTOBER 11, 1973

"Sweet Angeline," "All the Way from Memphis," "Rock and Roll Queen," "Rose," "Sweet Jane," "All the Young Dudes."

PAUL McCARTNEY AND WINGS

FORMED 1971

BAND MEMBERS WHO MATTER

Paul McCartney (lead songwriter, lead vocals, bass and assorted instruments), Linda McCartney (contributing songwriter, keyboards, vocals), Denny Laine (guitar, bass, vocals, contributing songwriter), Denny Seiwell (drums, percussion), Henry McCullough (guitar, vocals), Jimmy McCulloch (guitar, vocals), Joe English (drums, percussion).

> *THE CHRIS FARLEY SHOW:* Remember when you were with the Beatles? That was awesome...

WHY THEY MATTER

...And so went one of the funniest *Saturday Night Live* sketches (1993) where guest Paul McCartney played straight man to Chris Farley's buffoonish talk show character. In a way, Farley's question wasn't brainless. After all, it had been twenty-three years since the Beatles disbanded and life went on for the "cute one" (McCartney hated that description).

The 1970s was an eventful and prolific decade for the ex-Beatle, who settled into his own way of life and musical aspirations. But it was a challenging one with annoying questions about a Beatles reunion, his post-Beatles artistic credibility—and last but not least—Linda McCartney's musicianship (she was an accidental bandmate).

Paul McCartney.

DENNY SEIWELL: I really felt sorry for the kid [Linda]. There was more than one occasion when she broke down in tears and said "Denny, I don't think I can do this. Everyone hates me." But she had balls...and OK, she wasn't the world's greatest keyboard player but I had a lot more respect for her than plenty of other players I worked with. She was an awesome woman.

Linda McCartney and Paul McCartney.

Following the Beatles' breakup, Paul McCartney released two solo albums: the home-recorded *McCartney* in 1970 and *Ram* in 1971. Despite the cool reception, both soared up the charts and achieved platinum certification. The singles "Another Day" and "Uncle Albert/Admiral Halsey" (off *Ram*) connected with fans, but McCartney's pièce de résistance off *McCartney* was "Maybe I'm Amazed"—a thank-you to his wife, Linda, for helping him cope with the Beatles' breakup.

Macca then wiped the slate clean and formed Wings. The name was inspired by the complicated birth of Stella McCartney. The lineup included ex–Moody Blues guitarist Denny Laine and *Ram* drummer Denny Seiwell. Their studio debut *Wild Life* was a rush job that received brutal reviews. Before touring Europe, Wings added guitarist Henry McCullough (ex–Spooky Tooth, Grease Band) and embarked on a "tune-up" tour by van. They showed up unannounced at British universities. Keep in mind that McCartney hadn't toured for years.

PAUL McCARTNEY: The main thing I didn't want was to come on stage, faced with the whole torment of five rows of press people with their little pads, all looking at me and saying, "Oh well, he's not as good as he was."

Denny Laine.

Wings entered the studio and released three non-album singles, including the rocker "Hi, Hi, Hi." It was banned by the BBC for drug and sexual references. Renamed Paul McCartney and Wings (it gets confusing), the band released the 1973 LP *Red Rose Speedway*. Despite mixed reviews, the album was a commercial success (no. 1 in the United States) along with the orchestrated hit single "My Love."

During the making of *Red Rose Speedway*, the McCartneys and Wings went to the movies—figuratively speaking. Reunited with Beatles producer George Martin, Paul worked on the James Bond movie soundtrack *Live and Let Die*. The title track was a Top 10 hit both in America and the United Kingdom and remains one of the most memorable songs of the James Bond movie franchise.

Following a 1973 tour of the United Kingdom, Wings became a trio when Henry McCullough and Denny Seiwell departed. Paul, Linda and Denny Laine chose Lagos, Nigeria, for their next album. It was a poor decision: the government was a military junta, crime was rampant (Paul and Linda were robbed), cholera was breaking out and the studio equipment was faulty.

But the finished product—*Band on the Run*—was the group's most celebrated and commercially successful LP. It topped the charts in multiple countries and featured the timeless classics "Jet," "Let Me Roll It," "Band on the Run" (a Grammy winner), "Helen Wheels" and "Nineteen Hundred and Eighty-Five." The album silenced McCartney's critics.

In 1975, guitarist Jimmy McCulloch and drummer Joe English (who replaced Geoff Britton) joined the band. Once again, Wings struck platinum with *Venus and Mars*. It topped the charts in multiple countries. McCartney's sweet, optimistic love song "Listen to What the Man Said" was a no. 1 single in the United States and Canada. The anti-drug song "Medicine Jar" was co-written and sung by Jimmy McCulloch.

The momentum continued in 1976 with another chart-topping platinum LP, *Wings at the Speed of Sound*. The singles "Let 'Em In" (a shout-out to friends, acquaintances and relatives) and the nostalgic "Silly Love Songs" topped the U.S. Billboard and Adult Contemporary charts.

On May 3, 1976, Wings launched their only tour of North America with Paul and Linda, multi-instrumentalist Denny Laine, guitarist Jimmy McCulloch, drummer Joe English and a brass and reeds section. It was the first Wings tour to include Beatles songs. McCartney was proud of the tour. The resulting triple live package *Wings Over America* topped the charts in North America and was certified platinum.

McCartney and Laine then composed a surprising hit—complete with bagpipes. "Mull of Kintyre," a love letter to Scotland, became the best-selling non-charity pop single in British history. The song referenced a peninsula in Scotland where McCartney lived and sought solace following the Beatles' breakup.

Before the departure of guitarist Jimmy McCulloch and drummer Joe English, Wings released the commercially successful studio LP *London Town* and the single "With a Little Luck." The band's last gasp was the studio LP *Back to the Egg* with an impressive list of guest musicians.

In early 1980, Wings arrived in Tokyo for an eleven-date tour of Japan. McCartney's infamous drug bust ended the tour before it began. The shocking death of John Lennon gave McCartney further pause. He ended Wings in April 1981.

Jimmy McCulloch (*left*) and
Paul McCartney.

Paul McCartney.

The sales numbers and awards speak for themselves: McCartney and Wings (or just Wings) was immensely popular and successful. McCartney won over jaded and cynical Beatles fans and critics who initially frowned on his sentimental, middle-of-the-road pop songs.

PAUL McCARTNEY: I used to think that all of my Wings' stuff was second-rate, but I began to meet younger kids, not from my Beatle generation, who would say, "We really love this song."

In one of his final interviews, John Lennon remarked, "I kind of admire the way Paul started back from scratch, forming a new band and playing in small dance halls." Lennon understood the feat his former bandmate pulled off.

MUSICAL INFLUENCES WHO MATTER

Elvis Presley, Little Richard, Chuck Berry, Buddy Holly, Carl Perkins, Fats Domino, Wilson Pickett, the Everly Brothers, the Shirelles, Eddie Cochran, Fats Waller, Roy Orbison, the Miracles, James Jamerson, Brian and Carl Wilson, Stevie Wonder, John Lennon, George Harrison, Ringo Starr, Django Reinhardt, Stéphane Grappelli.

PROBABLE CONCERT SETLIST:
CHICAGO STADIUM, JUNE 1, 1976

"Venus and Mars," "Rock Show," "Jet," "Let Me Roll It," "Spirits of Ancient Egypt," "Medicine Jar," "Maybe I'm Amazed," "Call Me Back Again," "Lady Madonna," "The Long and Winding Road," "Live and Let Die," "Picasso's Last Words (Drink to Me)," "Richard Cory," "Bluebird," "I've Just Seen a Face," "Blackbird," "Yesterday," "You Gave Me the Answer," "Magneto and Titanium Man," "My Love," "Listen to What the Man Said," "Let 'Em In," "Time to Hide," "Silly Love Songs," "Letting Go," "Band on the Run," "Hi, Hi, Hi," "Soily."

GEORGE HARRISON

GUITAR, SINGER, SONGWRITER, MUSIC AND FILM PRODUCER, HUMANITARIAN, GARDENER

GEORGE HARRISON: The biggest break in my career was getting into the Beatles in 1962. The second-biggest break since then is getting out of them.

WHY HE MATTERS

Any discussion of George Harrison's significance must begin with the Beatles. He was a member of the most culturally celebrated and musically influential rock 'n' roll band ever. As he matured, Harrison's guitar playing, songwriting and musical influences gained traction and respect. His well-placed riffs were key components in many Beatles songs.

TOM PETTY: He just had a way of getting right to the business of finding the right thing to play. That was part of the Beatles magic— they all seemed to find the right thing to play.

Some of Harrison's songs are among the band's best, but his influence went well beyond songwriting. He developed a passion for Indian classical music and nudged the Beatles into new dimensions both musically and philosophically. With his twelve-string Rickenbacker, he created that "jingle-jangle" resonance that influenced other bands like the Byrds. He also developed a sweet-sounding slide guitar technique.

George was a prime example of how each member of the Beatles moved on to succeed and grow in different ways. He was the first Beatle to launch a solo album and tour. He pursued nonmusical interests that gave his life greater meaning. And he had the influence to recruit celebrated musicians for solo projects.

His post-Beatles career had both highs and lows. His first two solo albums (released prior to the Beatles' official breakup) barely left a mark on the public's awareness. He then scored no. 1 albums with *All Things Must Pass* (1970) and *Living in the Material World* (1972). There were no. 1 hits like "My Sweet Lord," and "Give Me Love (Give Me Peace on Earth)."

More accolades followed for his 1971 *The Concert for Bangladesh* performed at Madison Square Garden. Along with a concert film and DVD, the album peaked at no. 1 in the United Kingdom and no. 2 in the United States. Harrison gathered some of the top names in rock for this groundbreaking charity event: Ravi Shankar and friends, Eric Clapton, Leon Russell, Bob Dylan, Ringo Starr, Billy Preston and members of Badfinger.

In 1974, Harrison formed his own record label, Dark Horse. A rushed 1974 album of the same name peaked at no. 4 but received disappointing reviews, as did the supporting tour due to laryngitis. As he was always a hesitant stage performer, it took another eighteen years before Harrison toured again with help from Eric Clapton.

From 1974 through 1987, a musical weariness set in. Several subpar albums were released, but Harrison was fully engaged in nonmusical ways such as gardening, renovating his Friar Park estate, filmmaking, production work, spiritual pursuits, family life and racing. Much of his detachment from music can be traced to the 1980 assassination of John Lennon. The whole idea of fame made him feel unsafe.

A musical reemergence took place in 1987 with the help of friend and musician Jeff Lynne of the Electric Light Orchestra. The album *Cloud Nine* was a strong effort and yielded the no. 1 hit song "Got My Mind Set on You" and the popular "When We Was Fab" (a nod to the Beatles).

Harrison's next music project was his most enjoyable since going solo. He formed the Traveling Wilburys with Lynne, Bob Dylan, Tom Petty and Roy Orbison. The 1988 album *Traveling Wilburys Volume 1* was a commercial and critical success and won a Grammy for Best Rock Performance by a duo or group.

In the 1990s, Lynne worked with Harrison, McCartney and Starr on two new Beatles singles for *The Beatles Anthology* album: "Free as a Bird" (1995) and "Real Love" (1996).

Willie Weeks and George Harrison.

Harrison was diagnosed with throat cancer in 1997. Two years later, he was viciously attacked on his property by a deranged assailant. George's son Dhani believed the attack weakened his father's body and spirit and allowed the cancer to return. George Harrison died on November 29, 2001, at the age of fifty-eight. His ashes were scattered in several rivers in India.

After Harrison's death, Jeff Lynne and Dhani Harrison completed the posthumously released George Harrison album *Brainwashed*. That same year, Olivia Harrison, Eric Clapton and Dhani Harrison organized the *Concert for George* with some of Harrison's closest friends. In late 2011, Martin Scorsese—in partnership with Olivia Harrison—released the epic documentary *George Harrison: Living in the Material World*. It was nominated for several awards.

Harrison never lost his sense of humor—even when death was looming. In a 2001 Yahoo webchat, he was asked if Paul McCartney still "pissed him off." He replied, "I'm sure there's enough about me that pisses him off, but I think we have now grown old enough to realize that we're both pretty damn cute!"

MUSICAL INFLUENCES WHO MATTER

Lonnie Donegan, Elvis Presley, Chuck Berry, Carl Perkins, Bob Dylan, Ravi Shankar and other Indian classical musicians, Buck Owens, Buddy Holly, Chet Atkins, Duane Eddy, Eddie Cochran, Elmore James, Gene Vincent, Scotty Moore, Joe Brown, Andres Segovia, Eric Clapton, Alvin Lee.

PROBABLE CONCERT SETLIST:
CHICAGO STADIUM, NOVEMBER 30, 1974

"Hari's on Tour (Tom Scott & the LA Express)," "Something," "While My Guitar Gently Weeps," "Will It Go Round in Circles (Billy Preston)," "Sue Me, Sue You Blues," "For You Blue," "Give Me Love (Give Me Peace on Earth)," "Sound Stage of Mind," "In My Life," "Tom Cat (Tom Scott & the LA Express)," "Māya Love," "Nothing From Nothing (Billy Preston)," "Dark Horse," "Outa-Space (Billy Preston)," "What Is Life," "My Sweet Lord."

BOB DYLAN

SINGER, SONGWRITER, GUITAR, BANDLEADER, HARMONICA, PIANO

ROBBIE ROBERTSON: I don't think Bob ever wanted to be more than a good songwriter. When people are like, "Oh my God, you're having an effect on culture and society," I doubt he thinks like that. I think Bob is thinking, "I hope I can think of another really good song." He's putting one foot in front of the other and just following his bliss.

WHY HE MATTERS

For the first twenty years of his life, he was Robert Allen Zimmerman. To the Jewish community, he is welcomed by his Hebrew name. But to the world, he is Bob Dylan—the most important and prolific musical artist of the twentieth century.

Zimmerman was born in Duluth, Minnesota, but grew up in the mining town of Hibbing. While listening to records in his home and tuning in to distant radio stations, Zimmerman heard country music and rural blues that would change his life.

He played in bands at Hibbing High School before enrolling at the University of Minnesota Arts School in 1959. Following three semesters and performances in Minneapolis coffeehouses, Zimmerman journeyed to New York in hopes of meeting Woody Guthrie.

Once there, the fledgling musician was pulled into the Greenwich Village music scene and opened for bluesman John Lee Hooker.

On August 2, 1969, Zimmerman legally changed his name to Dylan. While performing in Greenwich Village, he was heard by the legendary talent scout, producer and musicologist John Hammond, who convinced Columbia Records to sign his discovery.

Dylan's self-titled debut album went mostly unnoticed. Despite this, Columbia stuck with the folkie, and that decision resulted in a fifty-year relationship.

His second album—*The Freewheelin' Bob Dylan*—offered a glimpse into the Bob Dylan to come. Upon hearing the song "Blowin' in the Wind," gospel legend Mavis Staples was astonished at Dylan's profundity: "He was a white boy who hadn't experienced the first-hand effects of racial discrimination." But Dylan was profound in more ways than civil rights.

> **PATTI SMITH:** There are so many roads to travel in approaching the songs of Bob Dylan—stirring songs of social injustice, bittersweet transition, veiled remorse, and mystical celebration. But there is hardly anyone who can rival him in the depth and breadth of his investigation of the expression of love.

From 1964 through 1969, Dylan made seven critically acclaimed studio albums overflowing with timeless songs. He had the attention of a generation who at times was challenged by Dylan's ever-evolving music. He grew tired of the "folkie spokesperson" role foisted on him. He told interviewers he was not political, topical or anyone's spokesperson.

> **JOAN BAEZ:** Bob is one of the most complex human beings I've ever met. At first I tried to figure the guy out, but I gave up. I don't know what he thought about. I only know what he gave us.

A watershed moment arrived in 1965 when Dylan surprised fans at the Newport Folk Festival. Supported by members of the Paul Butterfield Blues Band, he delivered an opening set that was electric and loud. To some, this was sacrilegious. Dylan responded to his two-faced naysayers (and possibly a particular woman) with the "middle-finger" song "Positively 4th Street."

On his 1965 album *Highway 61 Revisited*, the single "Like a Rolling Stone" clocked in at six minutes and redefined the radio pop hit. *Rolling*

Bob Dylan.

Stone magazine named it the Greatest Rock and Roll Song of All Time. That same year, Dylan hooked up with members of the Hawks, later renamed The Band. His relationship with musicians Robbie Robertson, Rick Danko, Garth Hudson, Richard Manuel and Levon Helm would continue into the 1970s.

By the middle of 1966, Dylan reached another musical milestone with the double album *Blond on Blond*, recorded in Nashville. It featured no fewer than six Dylan classics. That year, Dylan crashed his motorcycle near his home in Woodstock, New York. While recuperating from this near-fatal accident, he kept the tape recorder rolling at the Hawk's home studio. The result was a treasure trove of demos, alternate takes and songs meant for other artists. Bootlegged material was gobbled up by fans and eventually released legitimately as *The Basement Tapes*.

The following year, Dylan returned to Nashville to record the subdued *John Wesley Harding*, best known for "All Along the Watchtower." Two years later, he surprised many with the country-infused LP *Nashville Skyline*. It featured a duet with Johnny Cash and the hit single "Lay Lady Lay." Dylan's voice was surprisingly deep and mellow (he was no longer smoking).

During the 1970s, Dylan enjoyed three chart-topping albums, including *Blood on the Tracks*. The album's highlights were "Tangled up in Blue," "Simple Twist of Fate" and "Shelter from the Storm."

Dylan tossed fans another curveball. In the early 1980s, he proclaimed himself a born-again Christian. However, a more secular Dylan surfaced a few years later with the album *Infidels*. The critically reviewed but instrumentally strong album benefited by the talents of Dire Straits members Mark Knopfler and Alan Clark, ex–Rolling Stone Mick Taylor and reggae legends Robbie Shakespeare and Sly Dunbar.

Later in the '80s, Dylan found comfort and camaraderie in the Traveling Wilburys. He finished out the decade with the triumphant solo LP *Oh Mercy* produced by Daniel Lanois.

In 1997, Dylan released *Time Out of Mind*, his first album of original songs in seven years. It won a Grammy Award for Album of the Year.

Dylan remained prolific, relevant and fresh in the new millennium. He enjoyed two no. 1 albums: *Modern Times* (2006) and *Together Through Life* (2009). He became the first musician to receive the Nobel Prize in Literature. He recorded albums that explored the great American songbook, the influence of Sinatra and some early Dylan songs reimagined.

In 2020, Universal Music bought Dylan's songwriting catalogue (over six hundred songs recorded by others more than six thousand times) for an estimated $300 million. Two years later, Sony Music bought Dylan's entire music catalogue, worth $200 million.

Not exactly chopped liver for a man whose idiosyncratic voice would likely be laughed off today's music and talent reality TV programs.

MUSICAL INFLUENCES WHO MATTER

Little Richard, Woody Guthrie, Lonnie Johnson, the Beatles, the Byrds, Hank Williams, Johnny Cash, Buddy Holly, Robert Johnson, Odetta, Chuck Berry, Roy Orbison, the Carter Family, Pete Seeger, Gene Vincent, John Lee Hooker, Lightnin' Hopkins, Dave Van Ronk, Joan Baez, the Flying Burrito Brothers, Aaron Neville.

PROBABLE CONCERT SETLIST: (DYLAN WITH THE BAND), CHICAGO STADIUM, JANUARY 3, 1974

"Hero Blues," "Lay Lady Lay," "Tough Mama," "The Night They Drove Old Dixie Down," "Stage Fright," "Share Your Love With Me," "It Ain't Me Babe," "Leopard-Skin Pill-Box Hat," "All Along the Watchtower," "Holy Cow," "King Harvest (Has Surely Come)," "Ballad of a Thin Man," "Up on Cripple Creek," "I Don't Believe You (She Acts Like We Never Have Met)," "The Times They Are A-Changin'," "The Lonesome Death of Hattie Carroll," "Nobody 'Cept You," "It's Alright, Ma (I'm Only Bleeding)," "Life Is a Carnival," "The Shape I'm In," "When You Awake," "Rag Mama Rag," "Forever Young," "Something There Is About You," "Like a Rolling Stone," "The Weight," "Most Likely You Go Your Way and I'll Go Mine."

STEPHEN STILLS

GUITAR, SINGER, SONGWRITER, BASS, BANJO, DOBRO, DRUMS, KEYBOARDS, ARRANGER

STEPHEN STILLS: I don't set out to write a political song. I am not one of those that feels compelled to write about what's going on. [But] if the material is there, I have to pick up an instrument and [get] a sense of melody; a feeling; and a snatch of a phrase; and you're off to the races.

WHY HE MATTERS

Born on January 3, 1945, in Dallas, Texas, Stephen Stills has been one of the most gifted musicians in American rock music history. He broke new musical ground with bands like Buffalo Springfield; Crosby, Stills, Nash (and Young); and Manassas. He's a two-time Rock & Roll Hall of Famer (Buffalo Springfield and CSN) and a member of the Songwriters Hall of Fame. And Stills is among the few to have played four of America's most defining music festivals: Monterey Pop, Woodstock, Altamont and Live Aid.

On his own, the multi-instrumentalist has tapped a large network of musician friends to distinguish himself as a solo artist. He has earned accolades for his rhythm, lead and fingerpicking styles on electric and acoustic guitars, banjo and Dobro. His ability to write music, arrange and play bass and keyboards earned him the nickname "Captain Manyhands."

While in his prime, Stills possessed a vocal range that could jump from sweet to surly with a falsetto thrown in for good measure. But Stills is modest about his ability to write lyrics.

Stephen Stills.

STEPHEN STILLS: [I'm not] Dylan, you know. I haven't got the gift of the language in my opinion although I've written some really nice phrases. Neil Young is a great lyricist. If you really wanted to hear some great songs, Neil Young would write the words and I'd write the music.

With his father's military ties, Stephen's family moved often. He was exposed to a variety of cultures and music, having lived in Texas, Louisiana, Central Florida and Costa Rica. After dropping out of college, he headed for New York and joined the vibrant Greenwich Village music scene, where he joined a group called the Au Go-Go Singers with Richie Furay, a future member of Buffalo Springfield.

During a tour of Canada, Stills met native Ontarian Neil Young. Through a series of chance Los Angeles encounters, Stills, Young and Furay formed Buffalo Springfield with Bruce Palmer on bass and Dewey Martin on drums. Formed in 1966, the quintet gained national attention with Still's song "For What It's Worth."

The Rock & Roll Hall of Fame credited Buffalo Springfield with "laying the groundwork for the folk-rock and country-rock genres" that followed. Following three albums and personnel changes, the band dissolved in 1968.

Stills then accepted an offer to lay down lead guitar tracks for an important period album titled *Super Session*. Conceived as a two-day jam session, the 1968 release was spearheaded by keyboardist, guitarist and music impresario Al Kooper. When Chicago blues guitarist Mike Bloomfield was unable to complete the sessions, Kooper recruited Stills for his guitar skills.

More serendipity would shape Still's career. David Crosby left the Byrds, and Graham Nash exited The Hollies. The Laurel Canyon neighborhood of Los Angeles was home to a collective of musicians and bohemian types. With Cass Elliot as the scene's unofficial concierge, Crosby, Stills and Nash came together.

Their 1969 debut LP *Crosby, Stills and Nash* ushered in a new singer-songwriter sound with beautifully woven harmonies not heard since the Beatles. With the urging of Atlantic Records chief Ahmet Ertegun, the trio became a quartet. Neil Young joined in time for the Woodstock Festival. Several acclaimed albums followed, but the decades-long collaboration would be pulled in several directions leading to a lifelong cycle of splitting up and regrouping.

GRAHAM NASH: We were our worst enemy. Put the four of us into a room and anything could trigger a fatal blast.

Throughout his long association with Crosby, Nash and Young, Stills forged ahead with other musical partners. In 1970, he released the highly successful and critically acclaimed solo album *Stephen Stills*. It was an authentic and masterful mix of electric and acoustic rock, blues and gospel with guest artists Eric Clapton, Jimi Hendrix and Ringo Starr. The album *Stephen Stills II* followed.

A year later, Stills assembled an impressive group of musicians capable of performing many styles of music. Named Manassas, the band's 1972 self-titled debut remains one of the pinnacles of Stills's career. A second album followed, but the group disbanded after two years.

In 2013, Stills formed a blues-rock group named the Rides with guitarist Kenny Wayne Shephard and legendary blues keyboardist Barry Goldberg. The Rides released albums in 2013 and 2016. Stills retired from touring in 2023 but remains involved in a number of noble causes.

MUSICAL INFLUENCES WHO MATTER

Chet Atkins, Duane Eddy, Jimi Hendrix, Eric Clapton, Jimmy Page, Jeff Beck, Chuck Berry, Lightning Hopkins, Richie Havens, Fred Neil, the Beatles.

PROBABLE CONCERT SETLIST: AUDITORIUM THEATRE, MARCH 9, 1974

"Wooden Ships," "Four Days Gone," "Jet Set (Sigh)," "Rocky Mountain Way," "Special Care," "Change Partners," "Cross Road Blues / You Can't Catch Me," "Everybody's Talkin'," "4 + 20," "Word Game."

Grace Slick.

JEFFERSON STARSHIP

FORMED 1974

BAND MEMBERS WHO MATTER

Paul Kantner (rhythm guitar, vocals), Grace Slick (lead vocals, keyboards, recorder), "Papa" John Creach (fiddle), David Freiberg (bass, keyboards, vocals), Craig Chaquico (lead guitar, vocals), Marty Balin (lead vocals), Mickey Thomas (lead vocals), John Barbata (drums), Pete Sears (bass, keyboards, guitar, vocals), Aynsley Dunbar (drums).

> **GRACE SLICK:** In 1978, Jefferson Starship was bound for a European tour. [Members suggested] let's bring the wives! Mothers! Children! Oh boy! Arghh. My idea of hell.

WHY THEY MATTER

Paul Kantner called San Francisco "forty-nine square miles surrounded by reality." From 1965 through 1970, the San Francisco Bay area was a magnet for like-minded youth celebrating artistic expression and new forms of music pioneered by bands like the Jefferson Airplane (Rock & Roll Hall of Fame inductees and winners of a Grammy Lifetime Achievement Award).

The Airplane was the first San Franciso Bay area band to land a major recording contract and attain commercial success. And so began the musical franchise associated with flight: Jefferson Airplane (1965), Jefferson Starship

(1974) and Starship (1985). The first two entities were closely linked, whereas the third was far removed musically and philosophically.

In 1970, the Airplane hit turbulence, and the seeds of the Jefferson Starship were planted with the cerebral sci-fi album *Blows Against the Empire*. It was essentially a Paul Kantner solo album made with musicians from the Grateful Dead and Crosby, Stills and Nash. The album was billed *Paul Kantner and Jefferson Starship* and marked the first use of the "Starship" moniker.

By 1972, the Jefferson Airplane had taken its final flight. Legalities required that the Airplane portion of the band name be dropped and replaced by Starship—a nod to the future.

In 1974, the Jefferson Starship launched. Their debut album *Dragonfly* included former Jefferson Airplane members Paul Kantner, Grace Slick, Marty Balin and "Papa" John Creach. New members were multi-instrumentalist David Freiberg (ex–Quicksilver Messenger Service), John Barbata (ex-Turtles, CSN), bassist Peter Kaukonen (Jorma's brother) and twenty-year-old guitarist Craig Chaquico. Peter Kaukonen was quickly replaced by British multi-instrumentalist Pete Sears.

Dragonfly was the first of Jefferson Starship's five gold and three platinum recordings along with twelve Top 40 singles. The band continued its evolution from hippie revolutionaries to more polished, middle-of-the-road rockers with its first no. 1 album *Red Octopus*. The album spawned the Jefferson Starship's highest-charting single, "Miracles," showcasing Marty Balin's distinctive tenor and romantic ballads.

> **PAUL KANTNER:** "Miracles" was a lovely song and unique for that time period. But from then on, we sort of got typecast as wimp rockers. RCA wanted more songs like "Miracles."

By mid-1979, Slick, Balin and Barbata had departed for myriad reasons, and the Jefferson Starship regrouped with singer Mickey Thomas and British drummer Aynsley Dunbar. Thomas possessed a sonic, soaring soprano similar to Steve Perry of Journey. Guitarist Craig Chaquico viewed Thomas as a fresh beginning.

With Thomas taking lead vocal duties, Jefferson Starship recorded *Freedom at Point Zero* (Top 10) and the hit single "Jane." But critics called the band's sound too slick and similar to Foreigner, Journey and Boston. Everyone but Paul Kantner was happy with the band's new direction.

Grace Slick returned, and the band recorded *Modern Times* in 1981. The LP featured the Top 40 song "Find Your Way Back." Guitarist Craig

Craig Chaquico.

Chaquico told *Creem* magazine, "We had to find out if [Grace] was serious about sticking around. When she started singing and harmonizing with Mickey, it was natural that she should be there."

Although Grace could be highly unpredictable, she was a gifted singer and songwriter. She possessed a sarcastic wit, striking looks and distinctive contralto singing voice fortified by a killer vibrato.

From 1982 to 1984, Jefferson Starship recorded two final albums that broke Top 40 and went gold. Their final album, *Nuclear Furniture*, spawned two more hits: the chart-topping "No Way Out" and the Top 10 "Layin' it on the Line."

A disenchanted Paul Kanter left Jefferson Starship in 1984 and wanted the Jefferson Starship name retired. In 1985, the remaining members of Jefferson Starship agreed to perform under the single moniker Starship. The new band enjoyed considerable commercial success in the latter half of the 1980s and still perform under the Starship name.

Paul Kantner died in 2016, and legal entanglements regarding the use of the Jefferson Starship name (also still performing) are ongoing. But despite the complete metamorphosis from a band of hippie revolutionaries to 1980s power rockers, the confusing franchise associated with flight remains one of rock's most enduring and historic music-makers.

MUSICAL INFLUENCES WHO MATTER

The Byrds, Buffalo Springfield, the Beatles, Bob Dylan, the Rolling Stones, Cream, Peter, Paul and Mary, We Five, the Lovin' Spoonful, Skip James, Odetta, Kingston Trio, the Weavers, Howlin' Wolf, Muddy Waters, Sonny Boy Williamson, the Carter Family, Roy Acuff, Reverend Gary Davis, Otis Redding.

PROBABLE CONCERT SETLIST:
AUDITORIUM THEATRE, NOVEMBER 17, 1974

"Ride the Tiger," "Wooden Ships," "Papa John's Down Home Blues," "All Fly Away," "Sunrise," "Hijack," "Home," "Have You Seen the Stars Tonight," "XM," "Starship," "Milk Train," "Somebody to Love," "Volunteers."

THE MARSHALL TUCKER BAND

FORMED 1971

BAND MEMBERS WHO MATTER

Doug Gray (lead vocals), Toy Caldwell (lead guitar, pedal steel, vocals), Jerry Eubanks (keyboards, reeds), George McCorkle (rhythm guitar, banjo), Tommy Caldwell (bass, background vocals), Paul Riddle (drums).

> **PAUL RIDDLE:** Our musical backgrounds were so diverse that some would say that it made no sense at all. But that diversity really made it work. All the elements were perfect for the time.

WHY THEY MATTER

The music collectively known as southern rock was at its apex during the 1970s. Although the Allman Brothers Band (ABB) and Lynyrd Skynyrd immediately come to mind, others like the Marshall Tucker Band (MTB) distinguished themselves commercially and artistically. MTB's sound drew from guitar-driven rock, country (traditional and cowboy), jazz, rhythm 'n' blues and gospel. They played "country crossover" well before its advent.

For many years, Spartanburg, South Carolina, was home to an abundance of textile mills. In the late 1960s, it was also home to musically inclined young men like brothers Toy and Tommy Caldwell, Doug Gray, Jerry

Eubanks, Paul Riddle, George McCorkle and Franklin Wilkie. During their high school years, they played in bands and worked in occupations like plumbing, bill collecting and construction. Four of MTB's original members also served in the military during the Vietnam War.

But music was their ultimate calling. When they formed the Toy Factory, their fortunes began to change. During a club gig, they were discovered by Jimmy and Jack Hall of the southern rock band Wet Willie.

> **JIMMY HALL:** They just knocked us out from the beginning. [Their music] had a lot of the elements that were good old southern rock and rock 'n' roll. But there were so many things that set them apart from the others.

Once signed to Capricorn Records, the Toy Factory played clubs all over the South. Prior to making a record, Toy Caldwell felt the band needed a name change. While rehearsing in a warehouse space, they came across a keychain inscribed with the name Marshall Tucker—a blind piano tuner. Someone suggested using the name for a weekend gig, and it stuck.

In 1971, the boys caught another break when the Allman Brothers Band invited them as their opening act. Two years later, MTB began work on their self-titled debut album while living on cheese, crackers and booze. Their debut album *The Marshall Tucker Band* featured two classic songs: "Can't You See" and "Take the Highway."

Years later, "Can't You See" was named best southern rock song by the website Ultimate Classic Rock. Even the late Lester Bangs—one of rock music's most lauded but harshest critics—was impressed with MTB's debut. He wrote in *Rolling Stone* magazine, "If they're anywhere as good live as on this record, they could become very big indeed."

That part was quickly answered. By 1974, the band was playing three hundred or more dates per year and filling large venues. Tommy Caldwell was the band's leader and visionary, but brother Toy did most of the songwriting and was one of the most underrated guitarists of his era.

> **CHARLIE DANIELS:** Toy was half hillbilly, about a quarter jazz and a quarter rock and blues and stuff. But no matter how far out he'd get jamming, you could always hear those country licks in there. He was my buddy.

Toy Caldwell.

Tommy Caldwell.

From 1973 through 1980, the MTB released nine albums. Eight cracked the Top 40 (Billboard 200), and four made Top 40 on the country chart. In 1975, they scored their first Top 40 hit song with George McCorkle's "Fire on the Mountain," originally written for Charlie Daniels. Their 1977 album *Carolina Dreams* went platinum and spawned MTB's highest-charting single ever—the radio-friendly "Heard It in a Love Song."

In 1980, tragedy struck when bassist Tommy Caldwell died in a vehicular accident. The band voted to keep going and bring in friend and former Toy Factory bassist Franklin Wilkie.

As MTB's commercial success waned and Warner Brothers pressured the group to change direction, Toy Caldwell, George McCorkle and Paul Riddle departed. They agreed to let lead vocalist Doug Gray and keyboardist Jerry Eubanks carry on by purchasing the MTB name for performing and recording purposes. Thus began the next generation of MTB.

Jerry Eubanks retired from MTB in 1996, leaving Doug Gray as the only original member. Fast-forward to 2023. Gray told the website Taste of Country, "I don't think I have the ability to quit….I don't think that God wants me to quit." If that blind piano tuner named Marshall Tucker was alive today, he'd surely agree.

MUSICAL INFLUENCES WHO MATTER

B.B. King, Freddie King, Jimi Hendrix, Duane Allman, Robert Johnson, Hank Williams, Roy Acuff, Chet Atkins, Hank Garland and His Sugarfooters, the Ventures, the Beatles, Carl Perkins, Leslie West, Jimmy Nolan, King Curtis, Aretha Franklin, Dave Brubeck, Count Basie, Miles Davis, Buddy Rich, John Coltrane, Elvin Jones.

PROBABLE CONCERT SETLIST:
NORTHERN ILLINOIS UNIVERSITY (DEKALB, IL), DECEMBER 7, 1974

"Hillbilly Band," "Bound and Determined," "Searchin' for a Rainbow," "Can't You See," "24 Hours at a Time," "Fire on the Mountain," "Ramblin'," "Take the Highway," "Every Day I Have the Blues," "The Thrill Is Gone."

CHICAGO

FORMED 1967

BAND MEMBERS WHO MATTER

Walter Parazaider (reed and flute instruments), Terry Kath (guitar, lead vocals), Danny Seraphine (drums), Lee Loughnane (trumpet), James Pankow (trombone), Robert Lamm (keyboards, lead vocals), Peter Cetera (bass, lead vocals).

> LEE LOUGHNANE: In the swing era, horns were the vocals of the time. Our goal was to make horns the lead voice again in rock music, and we've been pretty successful at it.

WHY THEY MATTER

For over two hundred years, modern brass and reed instruments have shaped nearly every form of music, including rock 'n' roll. Along came the Beatles, and the rock music revolution embraced the amplified sounds of guitar, bass, drums and keyboards.

In the late 1960s and early 1970s, Columbia Records signed several acts that reestablished the role of horn and reed instruments in rock music. The Flock, Electric Flag, Buckinghams and Blood, Sweat and Tears received critical acclaim, but all were surpassed by their label mate Chicago—one of America's most commercially successful and longest-running bands to date.

The statistics bear this out: Since 1969, Chicago has recorded thirty-eight albums and sold well over 100 million records. They've racked up twenty Top 10 Billboard Hot 100 singles. Twenty albums have earned platinum sales certification. The band's 1969 debut album was inducted into the Grammy Hall of Fame. And for many, the band's 2016 induction into the Rock & Roll Hall Fame was too long in coming.

The concept of a rock 'n' roll band with horns sprang from the mind of founding member Walter Parazaider, who—at the time—was studying orchestral clarinet and English literature at Chicago's DePaul University. Parazaider sought out formally trained and street-credentialed musicians to act on his dream.

Joining were teenage friend and local guitar wizard Terry Kath; DePaul University student and trumpet player Lee Loughnane; and a local drummer named Danny Seraphine, who took private lessons at DePaul. The four called themselves the Missing Links.

Four grew to five with the addition of James Pankow, another DePaul University student, who excelled on trombone. Needing a keyboard player, the Missing Links found Robert Lamm, a Roosevelt University music student and jazz enthusiast. When Lamm was asked if he could play the bass pedals, he fibbed and said yes.

Robert Lamm.

Left to right: James Pankow, Walter Parazaider and Lee Loughnane.

For now, the band had a makeshift bass player. The sextet rehearsed James Brown and Wilson Pickett songs in Parazaider's parents' basement and renamed themselves the Big Thing. While playing regional gigs, they crossed paths with Chicago native Peter Cetera, who played bass guitar and sang in a Midwest club band. The six were now seven with a legitimate

bass player whose tenor voice added range to the baritone vocals of Kath and Lamm.

Enter James Guercio, another DePaul student, friend and musician. Guercio had connections with CBS (a division of Columbia) and became their manager. He moved the band to LA and changed their name to the Chicago Transit Authority (CTA). That name appeared on the band's first Columbia album but was shortened to Chicago for legal reasons.

WALTER PARAZAIDER: It was amazing because we were close friends. We had gone through this upheaval of leaving Chicago and moving to LA at a young age, leaving our families and just rolling the dice. We stuck close together and kept everyone's egos in check. The one thing that seemed to help us was our facelessness behind the logo.

Chicago's earliest albums blended psychedelic rock, pop, balladry, classical, jazz and rhythm 'n' blues. Terry Kath's scorching guitar (Jimi Hendrix was a fan) was prominent along with an abundance of extended jams, political messaging, soulful three-part harmonies and a triple brass attack.

By the mid-1970s, the enormously successful band moved away from its hard-driving, horn-propelled rock sound and turned to bassist Peter Cetera for radio-ready ballads like "If You Leave Me Now." Not everyone was pleased.

Transition and tragedy followed. In late 1977, Chicago split from friend and mentor James Guercio. On January 23, 1978, guitarist Terry Kath died from an accidental self-inflicted gunshot wound. Kath was Chicago's leader on stage. His deep, soulful vocals and avant-garde guitar outbursts were key elements of Chicago's early sound and appeal. His loss devastated band members, but the band continued on.

A resurgence followed in 1982. Chicago signed with Warner Brothers and, in 1984, released their best-selling album ever: *Chicago 17*.

LEE LOUGHNANE: We gained a new generation of fans. People would give an eye tooth for the amount of success we had in the 1970s and being able to do it a second time is a major milestone in the history of rock-and-roll.

More challenges followed. In 1985, original bassist Peter Cetera left to establish a solo career. Around 1990, Chicago parted ways with original drummer Danny Seraphine. Walter Parazaider retired in 2017. As of this writing, the band originally named after Chicago's public transit system plays on with originals Loughnane, Pankow and Lamm leading the way.

MUSICAL INFLUENCES WHO MATTER

Benny Goodman, Chicago Symphony Orchestra, Johann Sebastian Bach, Igor Stravinsky, the Beatles, James Brown, Wilson Pickett, Ray Charles, Art Tatum, Jimmy Webb, Jimi Hendrix, Sly and the Family Stone, Gene Krupa, Mitch Mitchell, Buddy Rich, the Beach Boys, Ventures, Dick Dale, Cannonball Adderly, Eric Clapton, George Benson, John Coltrane, Hal Blaine, Lester Young, Tony Williams.

PROBABLE CONCERT SETLIST:
CHICAGO STADIUM, JUNE 2, 1975

"Introduction," "Beginnings," "Old Days," "Does Anybody Really Know What Time It Is?," "Call on Me," "Anyway You Want," "Just You 'n' Me; (I've Been) Searchin' So Long," "Mongonucleosis," "Make Me Smile," "So Much to Say, So Much to Give," "Anxiety's Moment," "West Virginia Fantasies," "Colour My World," "To Be Free," "Now More Than Ever," "25 or 6 to 4," "Dialogue (Part I & II)," "Wishing You Were Here (with the Beach Boys)," "God Only Knows (with the Beach Boys)," "Darlin' (with the Beach Boys)."

THE DOOBIE BROTHERS

FORMED 1970

BAND MEMBERS WHO MATTER

Tom Johnston (guitar, harmonica, vocals), Patrick Simmons (guitar, banjo, flute, vocals), John Hartman (drums, percussion, vocals), Michael Hossack (drums, percussion), Tiran Porter (bass, vocals), Keith Knudsen (drums, percussion, vocals), Jeff "Skunk" Baxter (guitar, vocals), Michael McDonald (keyboards, accordion, vocals), John McFee (guitar, pedal steel, violin, vocals).

> PATRICK SIMMONS: There are no head honchos or driving forces in the Doobie Brothers. We're just a rock and roll band and as long as everybody shows up, we're still in business.

WHY THEY MATTER

In 1865, Wells Fargo built a stagecoach stop in the Santa Cruz Mountains of Northern California. Over time, it was also used as an outlaw hideout, brothel, speakeasy and French restaurant. In the mid-1960s, it evolved into a hippie and artist community, a watering hole for outlaw bikers and a music venue for area bands, including the start-up Doobie Brothers. Such was the evolution of the property named Chateau Liberté.

The band named for a marijuana cigarette (Patrick Simmons called it "the goofiest band name ever") has covered a lot of ground between performing

Bobby LaKind (*left*) and Patrick Simmons.

for the Hell's Angels and their induction into the Rock & Roll Hall of Fame. Their sustained success is even more remarkable considering the stylistic shifts and number of musicians who've contributed.

From the band's inception through 1975, the group was driven by the songwriting of Tom Johnston and Patrick Simmons. Their instrumental formula consisted of memorable lead and rhythm guitar hooks, multiple-part harmonies, a rhythm section propelled by two drummers and the playing agility of then bassist Tiran Porter.

From 1976 through 1982, the Doobies became a vehicle for keyboardist and blue-eyed soul baritone Michael McDonald, formerly of Steely Dan. When co-founder Tom Johnston was sidelined with a serious ulcer, McDonald was added on the recommendation of Doobie Brothers' guitarist Jeff "Skunk" Baxter—also a Steely Dan alumnus.

McDonald's smooth jazz, pop and white funk nuances widened the band's fan base, and even greater success followed. But the change alienated original fans. Johnston decided not to return until he reappeared for the band's 1982 farewell tour.

After a five-year break, the Doobies reunited for a charity event organized by drummer Keith Knudsen. The lineup included former band members with the exception of bassists Dave Shogren and Willie Weeks. The event turned into a mini West Coast tour that raised millions of dollars. Their shows at the Hollywood Bowl were the fastest sell-outs since the Beatles. The Doobies were back!

TIRAN PORTER: We had four drummers, four guitar players, two keyboard players and a percussionist and more. It was the most fun I ever had in that band.

Their legacy is rich in respect and recognition. They were inducted in the Vocal Group Hall of Fame in 2004 and the Rock & Roll Hall of Fame in 2020; have won four Grammys; and have sold an estimated fifty million records that include three multiplatinum, seven platinum and fourteen gold albums.

The band's catalogue of ubiquitous hits have stood the test of time: "Listen to the Music," "Long Train Runnin'," "China Grove," "Black Water," "Jesus is Just All Right," "Rockin' Down the Highway," "Take Me in Your Arms," "Takin' It to the Streets," "Minute by Minute," "You Belong to Me," "It Keeps You Runnin'," "Another Park, Another Sunday," "South City Midnight Lady" and "The Doctor."

Co-founder Tom Johnston offered a musician's explanation for the band's enduring appeal: "We're basically an American band. We cover a lot of areas: blues, rhythm 'n' blues, country, bluegrass, and rock 'n' roll. It's all based on rhythms, rhythm structures, picking and harmonies."

Multi-instrumentalist John McFee added, "We all have the same work ethic.…We are compelled to challenge ourselves. I mean, I love playing the old songs. But when we're working on new material now, I think we're coming up with better parts.…We're playing better than ever."

Jeff "Skunk" Baxter.

Fans and band members agree that the Doobies shine most brightly onstage. Tom Johnston confirmed: "The Doobies have always been about playing live. We're not a Studio Hothouse group or a concept album band."

A few years back, Patrick Simmons jokingly told an Ohio radio station, "We've been touring for what seems like one hundred years and it should end any day now." Well...not quite yet. The band led by Tom Johnston, Patrick Simmonds, John McFee and Michael McDonald are "Taking It to the Streets" (more accurately, the stage) once again in 2024.

MUSICAL INFLUENCES WHO MATTER

Moby Grape, the Allman Brothers Band, Freddie King, Chuck Berry, Little Richard, Bo Diddley, Elvis Presley, James Brown, Chet Atkins, Reverend Gary Davis, Mike Bloomfield, B.B. King, Doc Watson, Jorma Kaukonen, the Byrds, the Beatles, Bob Dylan, Carole Kaye, Jack Bruce, Dave Van Ronk.

PROBABLE CONCERT SETLIST: INTERNATIONAL AMPHITHEATER, NOVEMBER 25, 1977

"China Grove," "Takin' It to the Streets," "Sweet Maxine," "It Keeps You Runnin'," "For Someone Special," "Précis," "You're Made That Way," "Eyes of Silver," "Livin' on the Fault Line," "Little Darling (I Need You)," "Neal's Fandango," "Chinatown," "Long Train Runnin'," "Don't Start Me Talkin'," "Black Water," "Take Me in Your Arms (Rock Me a Little While)," "Jesus Is Just Alright," "Road Angel," "Listen to the Music," "Wheels of Fortune."

HEART

FORMED 1973

BAND MEMBERS WHO MATTER

Ann Wilson (vocals, guitar, flute), Nancy Wilson (vocals, guitar, mandolin), Roger Fisher (guitar), Howard Leese (keyboards, guitar, mandolin, producer, musical director), Steve Fossen (bass), Michael DeRosier (drums).

> **PEARL JAM:** Heart is our hometown [Seattle] band made good. They were the older kids from the Pacific Northwest who showed us where we could go if we wrote good songs, made records and toured hard.

WHY THEY MATTER

Heart was the first female-fronted hard-rock band to make it big when women were fighting for respect in a male-dominated industry. Their legacy includes ten platinum-selling albums (studio, live and compilation) and seventeen Top 40 singles, of which many are lasting rock anthems and power ballads.

Known as "Little Led Zeppelin" in their early days, the band originally named White Heart bounced around the clubs in and around Seattle and Vancouver, Canada. In 1972, Ann Wilson joined and fell in love with band

Ann Wilson (*left*) and Nancy Wilson.

member Mike Fisher (Ann's "Magic Man."). In 1974, sister Nancy joined the band and became romantically involved with guitarist Roger Fisher (Mike's brother). There was plenty of drama behind the music.

Early on, the Wilson sisters encountered sexism that would have derailed weaker types. But Ann and Nancy were strong women raised by a Marine Corps father.

> **ANN WILSON:** It took a long time for us to be taken seriously...to find so called credibility especially among the rock press. I remember hearing someone say, "That Nancy is a fine-looking girl, but is that guitar really plugged in?"

After making a demo, Heart was picked up by a small Canadian label named Mushroom. The band's 1975 debut album, *Dreamboat Annie*, was home to the radio classics "Magic Man" and "Crazy on You." The LP spent one hundred weeks on the Billboard Chart and showcased Ann Wilson's three-octave soprano that could fill large arenas or handle nuanced ballads.

With the band and album gaining traction in the United States, Heart asked to renegotiate their contract, but Mushroom refused. When Heart accepted an offer from another label, Mushroom released an unfinished version of Heart's next album titled *Magazine*. In a partial court victory, Heart won the right to have the rough album recalled, remixed and re-released. Despite concerns, *Magazine* sold and charted well and landed a Top 20 hit with the song "Heartless."

Heart's true second album was the impressive *Little Queen*, released in 1977. It went triple platinum in the United States and included the swaggering anthems "Kick It Out" and "Barracuda." The latter remains one of the best "take this, you sexist asshole" songs ever written. The song spoke to individuals at their former record company who "sexualized" the sisters in a promotion that fed media misogyny.

Little Queen also showcased Nancy Wilson's overlooked classical and folk guitar skills. Like her sister, Nancy possessed a magnificent voice, although softer and more subtle.

The band's streak of musically strong and commercially successful albums continued with their 1978 studio release *Dog and Butterfly*. An album of opposites, it included rockers like "Straight On" along with atmospheric ballads like "Dog and Butterfly."

Although Heart was succeeding musically, their romantic relationships were disintegrating. Roger Fisher was voted out of the band in 1979. Brother

Nancy Wilson (*left*) and Roger Fisher.

Mike (manager and soundman) soon followed. Roger Fisher's guitar duties fell to multi-instrumentalist Howard Leese and Nancy Wilson for the 1980 album *Bebe le Strange*. Although commercially successful, it was the first Heart album that failed to reach platinum status in the United States.

The 1980s marked a new beginning and change in personnel. *Private Audition* (1982) was the final album with drummer Mike DeRosier and bassist Steve Fossen. With Howard Leese as musical director, Heart added new members Denny Carmassi on drums and Mark Andes on bass. But musical tastes were changing. The music press labeled Heart a "dinosaur."

The Wilson sisters had no intention of going extinct. With new musicians and outside songwriters—Heart scored its first no. 1 album, titled *Heart*. It produced four Top 10 hits, including the chart-topping single "These Dreams" with Nancy Wilson taking lead vocals

Ann Wilson.

for the first time. Enter the MTV age. Industry suits were conjuring up misogynistic ways to best promote the attractive Wilson sisters.

> **NANCY WILSON:** We were not naturals to that way of doing things. We'd get stuffed into these awful outfits—tiny stiletto boots, corsets and bustiers. Shooting videos during that period could get pretty ridiculous.

The group closed out the '80s with two strong albums, but the formerly svelte Ann Wilson was gaining weight and raising concerns with Heart's record company. Ann and Nancy had enough and put Heart on hold. They formed the Lovemongers, an informal acoustic band with Sue Ennis—a longtime friend and behind-the-scenes music collaborator.

Howard Leese's twenty-year stretch with the band ended in 1998. In 2010 and 2012, the Wilson sisters returned to their "Little Led Zeppelin" roots with the albums *Red Velvet Car* and *Fanatic*.

Heart's well-deserved induction into the Rock & Roll Hall of Fame arrived in 2013. In 2024, the heart of Heart was still beating vigorously with the Royal Flush world tour. But as of this writing, European tour dates have been postponed while Ann Wilson undergoes treatment for a cancer diagnosis.

MUSICAL INFLUENCES WHO MATTER

The Beatles, Led Zeppelin, James Gang, Laura Nyro, the Rolling Stones, Joni Mitchell, Grace Slick, Paul Simon, Aretha Franklin, the Who, Neil Young, Jefferson Airplane, Crosby, Stills and Nash, the Guess Who, Free, Steppenwolf, Elton John, Deep Purple, John Mayall & the Bluesbreakers, Rod Stewart, Lucinda Williams, the Moody Blues, the Kinks, Eric Clapton, Richie Blackmore, Jimi Hendrix, the Beach Boys, Jeff Beck, the Ventures, Scotty Moore, Gerry and the Pacemakers, the Lovin' Spoonful.

PROBABLE CONCERT SETLIST:
INTERNATIONAL AMPHITHEATER, NOVEMBER 21, 1978

"Cook with Fire," "High Time," "Heartless," "Devil Delight," "Straight On," "Magic Man," "Love Alive," "Magazine," "Mistral Wind," "Dog & Butterfly," "Silver Wheels," "Crazy on You," "Kick It Out," "Barracuda," "White Lightning & Wine," "Rock and Roll," "Without You."

TODD RUNDGREN

MULTI-INSTRUMENTALIST, SINGER, SONGWRITER, BANDLEADER, PRODUCER, ENGINEER, MUSIC TECHNOLOGY PIONEER

TODD RUNDGREN: When I found out how easy it was to boost your ego by being a guitar player, I started looking for more challenging ways [to do so].

WHY HE MATTERS

Back when Todd Rundgren was a twenty-year-old member of the band Nazz, he told *Sixteen* magazine, "My ambitions, although not specific, are rather involved and would probably appear to most people to be within the realm of fantasy. I guess I'll just wait around and find out."

Find out he did. Todd Harry Rundgren has been hailed as a distinguished pop singer and songwriter, guitar hero, studio wizard, producer and technology innovator. His music has run the gamut from sublime pop songs to more adventurous works that have sometimes puzzled both his loyal fans (known as Toddheads) and the music press.

Among those he's produced and/or engineered include Badfinger, James Cotton, Meat Loaf, New York Dolls, Grand Funk Railroad, Patti Smith, Psychedelic Furs, Tubes, Alice Cooper and Hall & Oates. And last but not least, he tapped his "inner nerd" to develop new computer technologies and delivery systems for music and video.

Born of Swedish Austrian ancestry, the Philadelphia native grew up in a competitive family who expressed love sparingly. The guitar and music helped Rundgren build self-esteem.

Todd Rundgren.

After graduating high school, Rundgren played guitar in a local Philadelphia band named Woody's Truck Stop. When band priorities changed, he co-formed the band Nazz, named after a Yardbirds song. From 1967 through 1969, the British-styled garage rockers wowed Philadelphia teens. The experience gave Rundgren his first taste of stardom in addition to the highs and lows of the music business.

The musician nicknamed "Runt" headed to Greenwich Village, where he met Bob Dylan's manager Albert Grossman. Rundgren was hired as house producer and engineer at Grossman's Bearsville Records.

SALLY GROSSMAN: Todd was this boy wonder. To be such a renaissance man as he was at the age of twenty-one was very striking. His talent was already full-blown.

Yearning to make records on his own terms, he formed the band Runt. It was more a collective that served to launch his solo ambitions. Short-lived, Runt gave way to a full-blown solo career with a proliferation of eclectic albums beginning with the 1972 double LP *Something/Anything?* It became the most successful album of his career and a critically acclaimed masterpiece. He wrote, arranged, sang, produced, engineered and played every note on three sides.

The album yielded two beautifully written songs: "I Saw the Light" and a superior remake of the Nazz single "Hello It's Me." In 1981, Rundgren told Dave DiMartino of *Creem* magazine: "I was writing a song [a day] in 15 minutes. It became too easy. It was all formula essentially."

Fans and record executives wanted more of the same, but he disappointed his record label and fans with the follow-up album, *A Wizard, A True Star.* Then Rundgren changed directions again. He explained to Ron Ross of *Phonograph Record* magazine: "As soon as people start to expect something from me, I feel compelled to do something else."

Following another solo album, he returned to a rock band format. In 1974, he formed Utopia, a progressive rock outfit influenced by the bands Yes and Mahavishnu Orchestra.

TODD RUNDGREN: I created Utopia as a platform for me to become more of a guitar player and less of the kind of balladeer that people were taking me for.

During his on-and-off time with Utopia, Rundgren continued to make musically expressive and diverse solo albums along with other pursuits. The pop-accessible *Hermit of Mink Hollow* (1978) was his second-most-successful album. The single "Can We Still Be Friends?" was his first hit in several years.

In 1983, Rundgren's single "Bang the Drum All Day" became a cash cow. It is heard frequently at sporting events and in advertising campaigns.

The once gaunt-looking kid with distinguishing facial features has carved out a musical legacy minus the stardom. Patti Smith—who inducted Rundgren into the Rock & Roll Hall of Fame in 2021, said, "The fact that Todd did exactly what he wanted to and didn't bend to trends is admirable to me." Like Frank Sinatra, Todd Rundgren's epitaph will surely be "I Did It My Way."

MUSICAL INFLUENCES WHO MATTER

Jeff Beck, John Mayall's Bluesbreakers with Eric Clapton, Cream, Pink Floyd, Mahavishnu Orchestra, the Move, Yes, the Who, Laura Nyro, Carole King, Michael Bloomfield, Jimi Hendrix, Paul Butterfield Blues Band, Mose Allison, Marvin Gaye, Claude Debussy, Gilbert and Sullivan, Brecht and Weill, Richard Rodgers, Curtis Mayfield, Smokey Robinson, Sananda Maitreya, Stevie Wonder, Leonard Bernstein, Dionne Warwick, the Beach Boys, Robert Jay Bruner.

PROBABLE CONCERT SETLIST:
ARIE CROWN THEATER, NOVEMBER 17, 1973

"Le Feel Internacionale," "Never Never Land," "Long Flowing Robe," "It Wouldn't Have Made Any Difference," "I Saw the Light," "A Dream Goes on Forever," "Lord Chancellor's Nightmare Song," "Hello It's Me," "Piss Aaron," "Heavy Metal Kids," "Utopia Theme," "Black Maria," "When the Shit Hits the Fan / Sunset Blvd.," "The Ikon," "Number 1 Lowest Common Denominator," "Is It My Name?," "Hungry for Love."

Elvis Presley.

ELVIS PRESLEY

SINGER, ENTERTAINER, ACTOR

BRUCE SPRINGSTEEN: Elvis is my religion. If it were not for him, I'd be selling encyclopedias.

WHY HE MATTERS

The life, career and importance of Elvis Presley to rock 'n' roll remains impressive to this day. During his career, he set a new standard for career honors, hit songs and albums, certified record sales, concert attendance figures, television ratings, performance fees, fan worship, feature film appearances and controversary.

Elvis was among the most charismatic performers in popular music history. He delivered songs across multiple genres with a remarkable voice and natural sexuality that shook mainstream America. No one musician coalesced the power of rock 'n' roll quite like the "Hillbilly Cat."

AUTHOR MARTY JEZER: Elvis brought rock 'n' roll into the mainstream culture....Elvis, more than anyone, gave [youth] a belief in themselves as a distinct and somehow unified generation—the first in America to feel the power of an integrated youth culture.

Elvis Aron (or Aaron) Presley was born on January 8, 1935, in Tupelo, Mississippi, to a poor family during the Great Depression. His twin brother was delivered stillborn. With his family's deep religious convictions, Elvis was drawn to the music of his Pentecostal church. Hoping for a better life, Vernon and Gladys Presley took their thirteen-year-old son to Memphis, Tennessee—a musical melting pot of blues, rhythm 'n' blues and country.

In 1953, Sam Phillips—a small Memphis recording studio owner—ran a recording special: for about four bucks, anyone could put their performance on acetate. In walked a truck-driving teen with longish, slicked-down hair and colorful apparel. Phillips hooked Presley up with twenty-one-year-old guitarist Scotty Moore and bassist Bill Black. They made a demo of Arthur Crudup's song "That's All Right," which Phillips sent to a Memphis radio personality who spun it repeatedly. The station's switchboard lit up, and thus began the unofficial start of Elvis Presley's professional career.

On October 2, 1954, Elvis appeared at Nashville's Grand Ole Opry, but his performance fell flat with the venue's conservative audience. However, ensuing engagements at the competing Louisiana Hayride made Elvis a regional star.

ROY ORBISON: His energy was incredible, and his instinct was amazing. I just didn't know what to make of it. There was no reference point in the culture to compare it.

Enter the shrewd and manipulative Colonel Tom Parker—a Dutch-born entertainment impresario. The pros and cons of Parker's agenda have been long debated, but he helped make Elvis an international star and both men rich.

Parker bought out Presley's contract and music rights from Sun Records and sold them to RCA Victor, where Presley's sound rapidly evolved. In 1956, the future king of rock 'n' roll scored his first no. 1 hit with the moody and reverb-driven "Heartbreak Hotel." Presley was now defining the sound of rock 'n' roll.

His popularity intensified with a growing number of television appearances. But middle America—including old-guard entertainers and music critics—judged Elvis harshly. Although Ed Sullivan was among them, he understood ratings. To satisfy the censors, his cameramen shot Presley from the waist up. No swiveling hips.

By 1957, Elvis was a bona fide idol to millions of teens. He made news by purchasing a twenty-three-room mansion known as Graceland. A year later, Elvis was drafted into the U.S. Army and served eighteen months. While stationed in Germany, he met fourteen-year-old Priscilla Beaulieu-Wagner.

Elvis Presley.

During Presley's service period, RCA kept their star in the spotlight by releasing more hit material. But despite his success, Elvis was devastated when his devoted mother died just five months into his service.

Honorably discharged in 1960, Elvis headed to the studio and recorded two of his best-selling singles: "It's Now or Never" and "Are You Lonesome Tonight." Between 1960 and 1963, Elvis's music blanketed the charts, but from 1964 to 1968, his charting power declined as his film roles expanded.

Between 1961 and 1969, he knocked out twenty-five of his thirty-one nondocumentary films. Scripts were frequently formulaic, but his movies were a guaranteed box office draw and spawned hit songs and soundtracks. Several in his camp—including Elvis—felt his movie roles took a toll on his credibility as a musician. And with the arrival of the "British Invasion" and acts like Bob Dylan, Elvis was no longer cool.

But in 1968, his popularity returned when Tom Parker signed a deal with NBC for what became known as the critically acclaimed *Elvis Comeback Special*. A year later, Elvis signed a multiyear deal for a Las Vegas residency and, that same year, had his first no. 1 U.S. pop chart hit in seven years with "Suspicious Minds."

Although Las Vegas turned Elvis into a joke punchline, he could still draw. In 1973, he made history with four consecutive sold-out concerts at Madison Square Garden. That same year, his television special *Elvis: Aloha from Hawaii* was the first global concert beamed via satellite. It reached a staggering 1.5 billion worldwide viewers across forty countries.

Elvis won his third and final Grammy in 1974—all for gospel recordings. Presley gave his last live performance in Indianapolis on June 26, 1977. Troubles had long been brewing behind the scenes. On August 16, Presley's girlfriend found him slumped in a Graceland Mansion bathroom. He was only forty-two years old.

Elvis Presley endeared himself to millions and showed kindness through numerous acts of generosity. And he still lives on in popular culture.

In his book, Larry Geller, Elvis's longtime hairdresser, recalled the artist saying, "Ya know Larry, people call me The King…like I invented rock 'n' roll.…No way man. It all goes way back to the days in the old deep South. I mean, those poor people knew what real pain and suffering was all about. They used to sing and pour out their hearts to God just to get through the day."

MUSICAL INFLUENCES WHO MATTER

Roy Acuff, Ernest Tubb, Jimmie Rodgers, Jimmie Davis, Bob Willis, Jake Hess, Sister Rosetta Tharpe, Hank Snow, Dean Martin, Tony Bennett, Frank Sinatra, Perry Como, Arthur Crudup, Big Bill Broonzy, Howlin' Wolf, Sonny Boy Williamson, B.B. King, Rufus Thomas, Blackwood Brothers, Mario Lanza, Ike Turner, Eddy Arnold, Slim Pickens, Jake Hess and the Statesmen, Blackwood Brothers, Billy Eckstine, Bill Kenny, the Ink Spots.

Elvis Presley.

PROBABLE CONCERT SETLIST:
CHICAGO STADIUM, OCTOBER 14, 1976

"See See Rider," "I've Got a Woman," "Amen," "Love Me," "If You Love Me (Let Me Know)," "You Gave Me a Mountain," "Jailhouse Rock," "All Shook Up," "(Let Me Be Your) Teddy Bear," "Don't Be Cruel," "And I Love You So," "Fever," "Polk Salad Annie," "Early Morning Rain," "What'd I Say," "Johnny B. Goode," "Love Letters," "School Day (Ring Ring Goes the Bell)," "Hurt," "Love Me Tender," "Hound Dog," "Funny How Time Slips Away," "Mystery Train," "Tiger Man," "Can't Help Falling in Love."

MORE CONCERTS

Opposite, clockwise from top left: Dave Hill/Slade, October 16, 1973, Auditorium Theater. Steven Tyler/Aerosmith, October 11, 1973, Auditorium Theater. Jan Hammer, February 19, 1977, Auditorium Theater. Johnny Thunders/New York Dolls, October 11, 1973, Auditorium Theater.

This page, clockwise from top left: Left to right: Rickie Lee Reynolds, Jim "Dandy" Mangrum/ Black Oak Arkansas, July 30, 1974, Auditorium Theater. Steve Goodman, September 28, 1978, International Amphitheater. Jethro Tull, September 5, 1973, Chicago Stadium.

Opposite, clockwise from top left: Nils Lofgren/Grin, April 4, 1974, Auditorium Theater; John Sebastian, November 26, 1974, Auditorium Theater; Mick Grabham, Procol Harum, May 17, 1974, Auditorium Theater; Tommy Bolin/James Gang, February 22, 1974, Auditorium Theater.

This page, clockwise from top left: Paul Butterfield, March 30, 1973, Kinetic Playground; Diana Ross, January 27, 1977, Arie Crown Theater; Wet Willie, April 4, 1973, International Amphitheater.

Opposite, clockwise from top left: Robin Trower; James Dewar/Robin Trower Band; *Left to right*: Geezer Butler, Bill Ward, Tony Iommi, Ozzy Osbourne/Black Sabbath.

This page, clockwise from top left: Peter Gabriel/Genesis; Tommy Bolin/James Gang; Black Oak Arkansas with Larry Rosenbaum, Carl Rosenbaum and Howard Stein.

Opposite, clockwise from top left: Left to right: Dave Hill, Noddy Holder/Slade; Steve Winwood/Traffic; Nik Turner/Hawkwind; Lemmy Kilmister/Hawkwind.

This page, clockwise from top left: Cozy Powell/Bedlam; Pete Haycock/Climax Blues Band; Jeff Beck (*left*) and John McLaughlin.

BIBLIOGRAPHY

Album Liner Notes

Hip-O Records. *Martin Scorsese Presents the Blues*. 2003.
King, Freddie. *Freddie King 1934–1976*. 1977.
Nash, Graham. *Wild Times*. Atlantic Records, 1974.
Rolling Stones. *Get Yer Ya-Ya's Out!*. Decca Records, 1970.

Film

Pennebaker, D.A., dir. *Don't Look Back*. Leacock-Pennebaker Inc., 1967.

Books

Bashe, Patricia Romanowski, Holly George-Warren and Jon Pareles. *New Rolling Stone Encyclopedia of Rock & Roll*. New York: Fireside, 1995.
Benarde, Scott R. *Stars of David: Rock 'n' Roll's Jewish Stories*. Hanover, NH: University Press of New England, 2003.
Blaine, Hal. *Hal Blaine and the Wrecking Crew*. Chicago: Rebeats, 2010.
Buskin, Richard. *The Definitive Illustrated Encyclopedia of Rock*. London: Flame Tree Publishing, 2010.

Clapton, Eric. *Clapton: The Autobiography*. New York: Broadway Books, 2007.

Devine, Campbell. *All the Young Dudes: Mott the Hoople & Ian Hunter*. London: Cherry Red Books, 2007.

Klinger, Tony. *The Who and I*. New York: Gonzon Multimedia, 2017.

Marsh, Dave, and John Swenson. *The New Rolling Stone Record Guide*. New York: Random House/Rolling Stone Press, 1983.

Powell, Andy. *Eyes Wide Open: True Tales of a Wishbone Ash Warrior*. London: Jawbone Press, 2015.

Prato, Greg. *Bonzo: 30 Rock Drummers Remember the Legendary John Bonham*. N.p.: Greg Prato Writer, Corp., 2020.

Richards, Keith. *Life*. New York: Little, Brown and Co., 2010.

Schumacher, Michael. *Crossroads: The Life and Music of Eric Clapton*. New York: Citadel Press, 2003.

Shapiro, Harry. *Slowhand: The Story of Eric Clapton*. London: Proteus Books, 1984.

Slick, Darby. *Don't You Want Somebody to Love: Reflections on the San Francisco Sound*. Berkeley, CA: SLG Books, 1991.

Slick, Grace, and Andrea Cagan. *Somebody to Love? A Rock-and-Roll Memoir*. New York: Warner Books, 1998.

Strong, Martin. *The Great Rock Discography*. New York: Random House, 1998.

Szatmary, David. *Rockin' in Time: A Social History of Rock-and-Roll*. Upper Saddle River, NJ: Prentice Hall, 2000.

Whitburn, Joel. *The Billboard Book of Top 40 Hits*. New York: Billboard Books, 2010.

Websites

2011 Tribeca Film Festival Press Release | https://tribecafilm.com
977 FM Rock Station | 977rocks.com
ABKCO Music and Records | abkco.com
Alex Gitlin's Music Site | alexgitlin.com
All About Jazz | allaboutjazz.com
All Access | allaccess.com
All Music | allmusic.com
Alvin Lee: The Big Red Story | alvinlee.com
American Society of Composers, Authors and Publishers | ascap.com
American Songwriter | americansongwriter.com

Answers | answers.com
Anti-M | anti-m.com
The Aquarian | https://www.theaquarian.com
Associated Press | apnews.com
Atlanta Journal Constitution | ajc.com
Atlantic City Weekly | atlanticcityweekly.com
The Australian | https://www.theaustralian.com.au
AV Club | avclub.com
AXZ | axz.com
Bad Cat Records | badcatrecords.com
Bass Player | bassplayer.com
Bay Area Bands | bay-area-bands.com
BBC | bbc.com
Beatles Bible | beatlesbible.com
Billboard | billboard.com
Biography | biography.com
Blabbermouth | blabbermouth.net
Black Sabbath | blacksabbath.com
Blues GR | blues.gr
BMI | bmi.com
Brainy Quote | brainyquotes.com
Brave Words | bravewords.com
Bravo magazine | www.bravo.de
Britannica | britannica.com
British Invasion | https://thebritishinvasion.org/about
Brit Rock by the Bay | britrockbythebay.blogspot.com
Carl Palmer | carlpalmer.com
CBS News | https://www.cbsnews.com
CD Universe | https://cduniverse.com
Charlotte Observer | https://www.charlotteobserver.com
Chicago Reader | https://chicagoreader.com
Chicago Sun Times | suntimes.com
Chicago the Band | https://chicagotheband.com
Chicago Tribune | https://www.chicagotribune.com
Clash | https://www.clashmusic.com
Classic Bands | classicbands.com
Classic Rock | https://www.loudersound.com/classic-rock
Classic Rock Music Reporter | https://www.classicrockmusicwriter.com
Classic Rock Revisited | https://www.classicrockrevisited.com

Cleveland Scene | https://www.clevescene.com

Climax Blues Band | https://climaxbluesband.com

Columbus Ohio Public Radio | https://www.wcbe.org

Crossroads Centre Antigua. https://crossroadsantigua.org

Cryptic Rock | https://crypticrock.com

Culture | https://culture.org

Daily Mail | https://www.dailymail.co.uk/ushome/index.html

Danny Klein's Full House | https://www.dannykleinsfullhouse.com

Dan Pinto | http://danpintomusic.com

Dave Davies | https://www.davedavies.com

Dave Emlen's Unofficial Kinks Web Site | https://kindakinks.net

Dave Mason | https://www.davemasonmusic.com

Deadspin | https://deadspin.com/locker/

DGM Live | https://www.dgmlive.com

Digital Dream Door | https://digitaldreamdoor.com

Dinosaur Rock Guitar | http://dinosaurrockguitar.com

Discogs | https://www.discogs.com

Dissent magazine | https://www.dissentmagazine.org

DME Let It Rock | https://dmme.net

Doobie Brothers | https://thedoobiebrothers.com

DownBeat | https://www.downbeat.com

Down the Lane | http://www.downthelane.net

DPRP | https://dprp.net

drmusic | https://drmusic.org

Earcandy magazine | http://earcandymag.com

East Meets West Music | https://eastmeetswestmusic.com

Easy Reader & Peninsula | https://easyreadernews.com

Edgar Winter | https://edgarwinter.com/home/

Elephant Talk | http://elephant-talk.com/wiki/Fripp_Posts

Elsewhere magazine | https://www.elsewhere.co.nz

Elvis | https://www.shopelvis.com/store

Elvis Australia | biography.elvis.com.au

Emerson, Lake and Palmer | https://www.emersonlakepalmer.com

Encyclopaedia Metallum | https://www.metal-archives.com

Encyclopedia | https://www.encyclopedia.com

Entertainment Weekly | https://ew.com

Eric Clapton | https://ericclapton.com

Eric Clapton, Life & Music of a Legend | http://eric-clapton.co.uk

Facebook | https://www.facebook.com
The Famous People | https://www.thefamouspeople.com
Far Out | https://faroutmagazine.co.uk
Fly Guitars | https://www.flyguitars.com
Foghat | https://foghat.com
For Bass Players Only | http://forbassplayersonly.com
Forbes | https://www.forbes.com
Frank Zappa & the Mothers of Invention | https://www.zappa.com/#/
Fun Trivia | https://www.funtrivia.com
GBH | https://www.wgbh.org
George Harrison | https://www.georgeharrison.com
Get Ready to Rock! | https://getreadytorock.me.uk/blog/
Gibson | https://www.gibson.com/en-US/
Glide magazine | https://glidemagazine.com
Globalia | https://globalia.net
Golden Earring | https://golden-earring.nl/?lang=en
Goldmine magazine | https://www.goldminemag.com
Goodreads. "Popular Quotes." https://www.goodreads.com/quotes
Go Upstate | https://www.goupstate.com
Guardian | https://www.theguardian.com/us
Guitar | https://guitar.com
Guitar Player magazine | https://www.guitarplayer.com
Guitars International | https://www.guitarsint.com
Guitar World magazine | https://www.guitarworld.com
Heart | https://www.heart-music.com
The Heart Gallery | https://theheartgallery.net
HippieGirl | http://hippierefugee.blogspot.com
Hit Channel | https://hit-channel.com
HNGN | https://www.hngn.com
Hollywood Reporter | https://www.hollywoodreporter.com
Hood County News | https://www.hcnews.com
HubPages | https://discover.hubpages.com
HuffPost | https://www.huffpost.com
Ian McLagan | http://www.ianmclagan.com
I Love Manchester | https://ilovemanchester.com
In Music We Trust | http://inmusicwetrust.com
Innerviews | https://www.innerviews.org
Innovative Entertainment | associatedentertainment.com

Internet Movie Database | https://www.imdb.com
Interview magazine | https://www.interviewmagazine.com
In the Studio | https://www.inthestudio.net
Irish Times | https://www.irishtimes.com
iTunes | https://www.apple.com/itunes
JamBase | https://www.jambase.com
JAM magazine | https://jammagazineblog.wordpress.com
Jeff Beck | http://www.jeffbeck.com
Jefferson Airplane | https://jeffersonairplane.com
Jewish Telegraphic Agency | https://www.jta.org
Jim Capaldi | https://www.jimcapaldi.com
Jim Newsom and the Cloudless Sky | http://www.jimnewsom.com
Joe Cocker | https://www.cocker.com
Joe Walsh Online | http://joewalshonline.com
John McLaughlin | https://www.johnmclaughlin.com
Justin Hayward | https://justinhayward.com
Kast Off Kinks | http://kastoffkinks.co.uk
Kevin Hughes | http://kevinhughesmusic.com
Keyboard magazine | https://www.musicradar.com/keyboardmag
The Kinks | https://thekinks.info
K-SHE-95 | https://www.kshe95.com
KV2 Audio | https://www.kv2audio.com
La Music Blog | https://lamusicblog.com
Lancashire Post | lep.co.uk
last.fm | https://www.last.fm
Las Vegas Review-Journal | https://www.reviewjournal.com
Las Vegas Sun | https://lasvegassun.com
Legacy | https://www.legacyrecordings.com
Leo Lyons | http://leolyons.org
Leon Russell | https://www.leonrussell.com
Life magazine | https://www.life.com
Live Nation Entertainment | https://www.livenationentertainment.com
Los Marañones | http://donlope.net
Louder | https://www.loudersound.com
Loudwire | https://loudwire.com
Lovely Liv Tyler | https://www.lovelylivtyler.com
Lyrics Freak | https://www.lyricsfreak.com
Magical Moment Photos | https://magicalmomentphotos.com
Manticore Records | https://www.manticorerecords.com

Markvansch | https://markvansch.wordpress.com
Marshall Tucker Band | https://www.marshalltucker.com
Martin Turner | https://www.martinturnermusic.com/martin-turner
Mersey Beat | http://triumphpc.com/mersey-beat/
Metal Rules | https://www.metal-rules.com
Metal Storm | https://metalstorm.net/home/
Mike Pinder | http://www.mikepinder.com
Miles Copeland | https://milescopeland.com
Modern Drummer | https://www.moderndrummer.com
Mojo | https://www.mojo4music.com
Moments by Moser | http://momentsbymoser.blogspot.com
Moody Blues | https://www.moodybluestoday.com
Mott The Hoople and Ian Hunter | http://www.hunter-mott.com
Mountain Jackpot News | https://www.mountainjackpot.com
MusicBanter | https://www.musicbanter.com
Musicguy247 | https://musicguy247.typepad.com
Musician magazine | https://www.preservationsound.com/2011/03/
    musician-magazine-1976-1999/
Music-Illuminati | http://music-illuminati.com
Music Industry Blog | https://musicindustryblog.wordpress.com/category/
    artists-direct/
Musicmirror | http://musicmirror.de
Music Radar | https://www.musicradar.com
Music Row | https://musicrow.com
Music Web Express 3000 | https://mwe3.com
My Global Mind | http://myglobalmind.com
My Northwest | https://mynorthwest.com
Nashville Scene | https://www.nashvillescene.com
Newtown Bee | Newtownbee.com
New Yorker | https://www.newyorker.com
New York Times | https://www.nytimes.com
Night Flight | https://nightflightofficial.com
No Depression | https://www.nodepression.com
NPR | https://www.npr.org
NU Country TV | https://www.nucountry.com.au
Oakland Press | https://www.theoaklandpress.com
Oklahoma Gazette | https://www.okgazette.com
100.7 WZLX Boston's Classic Rock | https://wzlx.iheart.com
Open Culture | https://www.openculture.com

Paste | https://www.pastemagazine.com
Pat Metheny | https://patmetheny.com
Paul "Blowfish" Lovell | https://punkblowfish.com
Paulick Report | https://paulickreport.com
Paul Rodgers | https://www.paulrodgers.com/home
Pennyblackmusic | https://pennyblackmusic.co.uk
Perfect Sound Forever | http://www.furious.com/perfect/index.html
Peter Frampton | http://frampton.com
Peter Wolf | https://www.peterwolf.com
Phil Collins | https://philcollins.com
Phoenix New Times | https://www.phoenixnewtimes.com
Piero Scaruffi | https://scaruffi.comgo
Playboy magazine | https://www.playboy.com
Pop-Break | http://pop-break.com
Pop Culture Today | http://popculturetoday.com
Pop Matters | https://www.popmatters.com
Procol Harum | https://procolharum.com
Prog Archives | https://www.progarchives.com
Prog magazine | https://www.loudersound.com/prog
Progressive Ears | http://www.progressiveears.org/forum
Progsheet | https://www.progsheet.com
Psychedelic Baby | https://www.psychedelicbabymag.com
Pure Southern Rock | http://puresouthernrock.com
Rate Your Music | https://rateyourmusic.com
Ravi Shankar Foundation | https://www.ravishankar.org
Reader's Digest | https://www.rd.com
Red Rocker | http://www.redrocker.com
Repertoire Entertainment | https://www.repertoirerecords.com
Reuters | https://www.reuters.com
Rhythm & Blues | blues.about.com
Rick Derringer | https://rickderringer.com
Ric Lee | https://www.ricleetya.com
Rock | https://www.liveabout.com/rock-4688276
Rock & Roll Hall of Fame and Museum | https://rockhall.com
Rock & Roll Hall of Fame Library & Archives | catalog.rockhall.com
Rock Cellar magazine | https://rockcellarmagazine.com/#google_vignette
Rock's Backpages | https://www.rocksbackpages.com
The Rocktologist | https://www.therocktologist.com
Rod Stewart | https://rodstewart.com

Roger Dean | https://www.rogerdean.com

Roger Fisher | https://www.rogerfisher.com

Rolling Stone magazine | https://www.rollingstone.com

Rolling Stones | https://rollingstones.com

Ronnie Montrose | https://www.ronniemontrose.com

Rory Gallagher | https://www.rorygallagher.com

Salon | https://www.salon.com

San Diego Union-Tribune | https://www.sandiegouniontribune.com

Savoy Brown | https://savoybrown.com

Sea of Tranquility | https://www.seaoftranquility.org

Seattle Music Insider | https://seattlemusicinsider.com

Seattlepi | https://www.seattlepi.com

Seattle Times | https://www.seattletimes.com

SF Sonic | https://sfsonic.com

Sheff, David. "Playboy Interview: Frank Zappa." *Playboy*, April 1993.
    https://www.afka.net.

Shout Factory! | https://shoutfactory.com

The Slant | https://vanderbiltslant.com

Slate | https://slate.com

Softshoe's Music Matters Site | http://softshoe-slim.com

Something Else! | https://somethingelsereviews.com

Song Facts | https://www.songfacts.com

Song Meanings | https://songmeanings.com

Songwriters Hall of Fame | https://www.songhall.org

Sound on Sound | https://www.soundonsound.com

Sound Spike | https://soundspike.com

Spin | https://www.spin.com

Sputnik Music | https://www.sputnikmusic.com

Starostin's Record Reviews | https://starlingdb.org/music/index_old.htm

Stephen Stills | https://stephenstills.com

Stereo Embers | https://www.stereoembersmagazine.com

Steve Hackett's Official Website | https://www.hackettsongs.com

Steve Winwood | https://stevewinwood.com

The Sun | https://www.thesun.co.uk

Super Seventies | https://superseventies.com

Swampland | http://swampland.com

Sydney Morning Herald | https://www.smh.com.au

Tales from Down the Front | https://ligger.wordpress.com

Telegraph | https://www.telegraph.co.uk/us/

Ten Years After | https://ten-years-after.com
Ten Years After: Alvin Lee | alvinlee.de
Ten Years After Now | http://tenyearsafternow.com
Thrasher's Wheat | http://thrasherswheat.org
Time | https://time.com
Trafficbeat | https://trafficbeat.net
Trouser Press | https://trouserpress.com
Tulsa World | https://tulsaworld.com
UCR Classic Rock & Culture | https://ultimateclassicrock.com
Udiscovermusic | https://www.udiscovermusic.com
UFO | http://ufo-music.info/band.htm
The Uncool | http://www.theuncool.com
Un-finished Side | https://unfinishedside.com
Unofficial UFO and Michael Schenker | http://ufo.dave-wood.org
Uproxx | https://uproxx.com/entertainment/
Urban Dictionary | https://www.urbandictionary.com
USA Today | https://www.usatoday.com
Vanity Fair | https://www.vanityfair.com
VH1 | https://www.vh1.com
Village Voice | https://www.villagevoice.com
Vinnie Moore | https://vinniemoore.com
Vintage Guitar | https://www.vintageguitar.com
Vintage Rock | https://vintagerock.com
Washington Post | https://www.washingtonpost.com
Where's Eric! | https://whereseric.com
The Who | https://www.thewho.com
Why It Matters | https://wimwords.com
Wikipedia | https://www.wikipedia.org
Wilson and Alroy's Record Reviews | http://www.warr.org/cgi-bin/
    randompickpan2.cgi
Winwood Fans | https://www.winwoodfans.com
Wishbone Ash | https://www.wishboneash.co.uk
Woodstock | https://www.woodstock.com
Woody Tone | http://www.woodytone.com
World Music Central | https://worldmusiccentral.org
Yardbirds | http://theyardbirds.com
Y!entertainment | https://www.yahoo.com/entertainment/music
Yes | https://yesworld.com

YouTube. "Frank Zappa—Lost Interview 1991." https://www.youtube.com.
————. "Jake Feinberg Show." https://www.youtube.com/user/
jakefeinbergshow.
————. "Living Legends." https://www.youtube.com/livinglegends.
Zappa Books | afka.net

ABOUT THE AUTHORS

Oak Park, Illinois native JIM SUMMARIA is a veteran rock concert photographer whose photos have been published in numerous books, magazines and CDs. His rock 'n' roll photos have been viewed at the Illinois Rock & Roll Museum and Hall of Fame on Route 66 in Joliet, Illinois; The Grammy Awards Ceremony; the Rock & Roll Hall of Fame Induction Ceremony; and the Victoria and Albert Museum in London, England.

He's had gallery showings at Hey Nonny in Arlington Heights, Illinois; the Arcada Theater in St. Charles, Illinois; and the Artspace Gallery in Elgin, Illinois. He is a contributing photographer to *Premier Guitar*, *Chicago Blues Guide*, *Good Times* (Germany) and *Penny Black* (United Kingdom) magazines. He is coauthor (with Mark Plotnick) of the book *Classic Rock: Photographs from Yesterday & Today* and coauthor (with Pat Williams) of *Pictures for Employee Publications*.

Along with Mark Plotnick, he cohosts the radio program *That Classic Rock Show*.

His lifelong passion for rock photography began as an eighteen-year-old photographing rock concerts with a Kodak Instamatic at a 1972 Rolling Stones show. Thrilled with his early efforts, he soon invested in a 35mm camera with a telephoto lens, and his photos improved. He took his Led Zeppelin photos to Flip Side Records in Arlington Heights, Illinois, to see if they would display them on their wall. After a couple more concert photo postings, store manager Rich Carlson asked Jim to be Flip Side's official photographer at shows they promoted (at the time Howard Stein Productions and later Flip Side Productions).

With the blessing of owners Larry and Carl Rosenbaum, Jim got backstage photo passes to some of the biggest concerts in the 1970s—a lot of fun for a nineteen-year-old. In 1979, Jim began his career as a commercial photographer, which he continues to this day. And by the way, he is still photographing rock concerts.

MARK PLOTNICK is a native of the Rogers Park neighborhood of Chicago. He earned a bachelor of science degree from Loyola University. His love of rock and blues music proved too distracting during his initial year at the Illinois College of Optometry. He left to briefly sell pianos and organs for the Lyon and Healy Company, where he met longtime friend Alan Day, a beloved piano and organ teacher.

In 1984, Alan and Mark coauthored *The Smart Money Shopper*. It got the attention of area newspapers, radio and television programs, including Oprah Winfrey's regional show. Lacing up Air Jordans on Oprah's feet was a moment Mark will never forget.

These experiences led to new careers, including copywriting, public relations, magazine journalism, marketing and market research that included the writing of widely consulted research studies for a variety of Fortune 500 companies and industries.

Recently retired, Mark draws from his years as a nonprofessional keyboard player and devotee of classic rock–era music to write about the music and performers he loves. In 2019, he coauthored *Classic Rock: Photographs from Yesterday & Today* with friend Jim Summaria. In March 2021, Mark and Jim began hosting a weekly hourlong program, *That Classic Rock Show*, and in 2024, became a concert reviewer for *Chicago Blues Guide*.

Mark lives in the northern suburbs of Chicago with his wife, Hope, and spoiled Senegal parrot Squeaky. The odyssey continues.

Visit us at
www.historypress.com